Getting a
Project Done
On Time

Getting a Project Done On Time

Managing People, Time, and Results

Paul B. Williams

American Management Association
New York • Atlanta • Boston • Chicago • Kansas City • San Francisco • Washington, D.C.
Brussels • Mexico City • Tokyo • Toronto

This publication is designed to provide accurate and authoritative
information in regard to the subject matter covered. It is sold with the
understanding that the publisher is not engaged in rendering legal,
accounting, or other professional service. If legal advice or other expert
assistance is required, the services of a competent professional person
should be sought.

Library of Congress Cataloging-in-Publication Data

Williams, Paul B., 1948–
        Getting a project done on time : managing people, time, and
results / Paul B. Williams.
            p.   cm.
        Includes index.
        ISBN 0-8144-0284-4
        1. Time management.   2. Industrial project management.   I. Title.
    HD69.T54W544   1996
    658.4'093—dc20   95-26228
                                                                          CIP

Printing number

10   9   8   7   6   5   4   3   2   1

To
Howard & Edna
For not giving up trying for a daughter after four sons

To
Brian, Emily & Dylan
For their convincing demonstration that love is an instinct

To
Liz
For life

Contents

Preface

The Top Ten Reasons to Read This Book

10. Organizations that are willing to allow hastily planned, poorly led projects weaken themselves and endanger employees by wasting precious resources.

9. Organizations that are flattening (e.g., through reengineering, downsizing, or rightsizing) will depend on projects and project leaders to get work done that was once handled by departments.

8. With rare exceptions, project prime movers believe that project meltdowns are the result of weak project leadership.

7. More than one lumpy project leadership performance can give you a reputation that will repel future project participants.

6. Project work is often disguised by the use of the word *team*; if you find yourself on or leading teams, you're probably working with others to complete a project.

5. The abilities that are required to organize and carry out successful projects will enhance other aspects of your job.

4. Leading successful projects is the best way to prove your promotability to the people who make those decisions.

3. The best way to promote effective project leadership is

to set examples that are so powerful and positive that others wouldn't dare do less.

2. Project leaders seldom get better until they know how to do it right.

1. If you're not getting better, you're getting worse as you get older.

About the Top Ten Reasons to Read This Book

10. Organizations that are willing to allow hastily planned, poorly led projects weaken themselves and endanger employees by wasting precious resources. Too many companies act as if project leadership, like meeting leadership, called for the simple extension of the skills that any manager or professional already possesses. As reasonable as that assumption may seem, it is false. Projects, which almost always involve brand new challenges, only succeed if the leaders anticipate needed information, prepare and deliver revealing questions, select and/or prop up participants, develop and communicate detailed plans, influence resisters, manage time and work, present project results, and remain relatively calm if the project is unexpectedly shelved. If the leader doesn't know that each of these skills is called for, if s/he doesn't have time to give each of these aspects of a project adequate attention, or if s/he doesn't know how to do one or more of them very well, the project suffers. And suffer it does. Think through the projects you've led or participated in. What percentage underperformed or failed outright? Sometimes the "suffering" comes in the form of missed deadlines, extra resource needs, marginal results, or—in extreme cases—no usable result at all. Stack enough suffering projects on top of each other and you'll end up with a suffering company.

9. Organizations that are flattening (e.g., through reengineering, downsizing, or rightsizing) will depend on projects and project leaders to get work done that was once handled by departments. Back in the porky ol' days of just-in-case hiring and head counts, a neomilitary style of top-down management took care of all but the most peculiar types of work. *Superiors* assigned work to their *subordinates*, and business proceeded as usual. Those days are gone forever. Mean, lean, and green hiring and head-count adjustments have thinned employee ranks to the point where old work practices simply can't handle the load. Where groups of employees were ready to handle issues in the past, companies now pull project teams together to address an issue and then disband. In the present and near future, projects won't be the exception, they'll be the rule.

8. *With rare exceptions, project prime movers believe that project meltdowns are the result of weak project leadership.* Whether the cause of project underperformance is due to unforeseen problems, participant delays, or miscommunication, the blame almost always finds its way back to the leader. Where else would it go? When a project prime mover authorizes a project, the leader is given time, a budget, and a measure of trust. Every extra dollar required to finish and every day required beyond the deadline come off the top of any glory the project leader would have otherwise earned. Explanations may be listened to politely, but don't kid yourself—they come off like excuses.

7. *More than one lumpy project leadership performance can give you a reputation that will repel future project participants.* It gets worse. Not only do underperforming project leaders lose points with management for blown schedules or budgets, they are also quickly identified by potential participants as frustrators and/or time wasters. Everyone has more work than they know what to do with, which means that many of them are bootlegging time from home, honey, and hearth. Waste their time and effort in an ill-planned or poorly communicated project and you will quickly find out what the new paradigm's version of *shunning* is.

6. *Project work is often disguised by the use of the word* team; *if you find yourself on or leading teams, you're probably working with others to complete a project.* Depending on the point of view of your organization, you may be leading or participating in a project and not even recognize it. Are you a team leader or a team member? In many cases, team is to project as cooking is to casserole. *Team* (a favorite word among extroverts) focuses on the activity and relationships while *project* (would the introverts quietly nod their heads) focuses more on the outcome. This

book, although its title indicates the word *project*, tries to find a common ground between these two points of view and, in doing so, include the best of both.

5. *The abilities that are required to organize and carry out successful projects will enhance other aspects of your job.* Successful project leadership is more about breadth than depth; as such, successful project leaders tend to be good at all aspects of their work. Planning, gathering information, influencing people, making use of your time, delivering effective presentations, and managing your own frustration levels are all part of being a strong project leader, an effective manager, a valued professional, and an irreplaceable individual contributor. If acted upon, the practical competencies detailed in this book could transform you into a Renaissance employee.

4. *Leading successful projects is the best way to prove your promotability to the people who make those decisions.* Ever wonder how you can get that next promotion in an organization that has fewer middle- and upper-management positions? If you're not managing now or if you're managing in a low-visibility part of the company, you may go for years before anyone notices your abilities—unless you make it a habit of leading highly successful projects. With business becoming increasingly competitive and cost-conscious, one of the very best ways to get noticed is to take the helm of a successful project. As you use the abilities outlined in this book to reliably bring in valuable results, opportunities will start knocking at your door.

3. *The best way to promote effective project leadership is to set examples that are so powerful and positive that others wouldn't dare do less.* A word of warning: You may be bucking tradition. When any organization tolerates the ever-worsening downside of project haste for very long, what was bad business practices can become an accepted standard in the culture. Lame justifications can appear ("We don't have time for much planning; we'll deal with it when we come to it!" or "Who has time to monitor other people's project work!") and be embraced as a potential excuse should disaster strike one's own project.

A word of encouragement: Buck tradtion! If, from the start, you invest time in leading projects right, you won't have to (1) spend time explaining what went wrong, (2) beg for additional help from misused participants, or (3) bootleg time from your loved ones so that you can make things right. Even better, you will begin to set a new standard for leading projects, and by raising the level of play within your organization, you will strengthen and enrich it.

2. Project leaders seldom get better until they know how to do it right. One of the great lessons of the past decade is that as a country, as companies, and as individuals, we can never rest on our laurels. There will always be someone gaining on us, which means that we must always strive to be better. Because project leadership is a key building block for producing value today and into the future, we must find ways to improve. For many—and perhaps for you—this book represents one of those ways.

1. If you're not getting better, you're getting worse as you get older. One last thought: You're lying on your deathbed and, as we know from the movies, your life is flashing before your eyes. In one scenario, that moment will be littered with bosses, co-workers, and legions of others complaining about how you wasted company resources, their time, and plenty of potential project enthusiasm by botching one project after another. In another scenario, you see legions of smiling faces thanking you for taking them to new heights of productivity and profitability. Of course, after your life finishes flashing, you'll expire, but which scenario would you prefer? The choice is yours.

Acknowledgments

This book has been profoundly influenced by the experiences and challenges of hundreds of managers from the JCPenney Company, where I teach a project management program. Without their insight, candor, tireless desire to improve, and clear competence, this book would have been impossible for me to write. A particular debt of gratitude is owed to Dan Zechmiester, whose ability, honesty, and upbeat attitude have made my association with the Penney Company a real pleasure.

Anthony Vlamis, Senior Acquisitions Editor for AMACOM Books, has been a joy to work with. Tony's humor, sensitivity, and guidance have been greatly appreciated and have done much to further the easing of tensions between New York and Texas.

During three years at the University of Oregon, my mentor, professor, and friend Zig Engelmann was a challenging and life-changing example of what a person can do if he decides to live the life he is given. Zig's genius for thinking and living continues to serve as an example and a kick in the pants.

John Lichtenthal spent hundreds of early-morning hours with me in a zealous attempt to collaborate on the definitive book about quality management. That book still resides in the ether of unwritten tomes, but the insights, ideas, and great fellowship we shared continue to influence my attitudes and actions.

Before anyone was even thinking about the new paradigm, Bill Evans helped me through the employee-to-stakeholder transformation with which so many present-day employees are struggling. Until I met Bill, I'd never seen anyone with the courage to work without a net and with the joy of life that is required to make it work. Without Bill's very timely influence, a great deal of my last dozen years would not have happened.

Finally, I would like to acknowledge my brother Tom. However, since mere words are not up to the task, I will simply hope that he knows how much he means to me.

Getting a
Project Done
On Time

Chapter 1
Fact Finding

Ready, Fire, Aim!

—Anonymous

Jack arrived at his workstation twenty minutes early, hoping to get a head start on his overgrown to-do list before the normal torrent of interruptions flooded his phone and E-mail. The blue Post-it note from Fran, his boss, caught Jack's attention immediately. "Come to my office ASAP" short-circuited Jack's early-bird plans, but he was resigned to the fact that at least for today, Fran was the real early bird and he was the worm.

As he waited for Fran to end a phone call, Jack marveled at how she could be so efficient in an office that had clearly grown too small for the books, papers, and equipment that filled it. Without Fran's uncanny recollection of every piece of paper in her pile-file system, her office could jump-start any high school paper drive. But Fran's memory, coupled with her drive, competence, and obvious leadership ability made her the best boss Jack had had in recent history.

Jack's thoughts ended abruptly as Fran looked up, waved him further into her office, and hung up the phone.

"Sit down, please," she said. "I need your help. Late yesterday afternoon, I met with three senior managers in Accounting. According to their best estimates, we've outgrown our inventory control software. With all the changes in accounting methods, warehouse locations, and computer hardware, the software you helped customize five years ago is hopelessly inefficient and is so difficult for our new employees to learn that we're unable to get product to our stores before they run out. And that doesn't even touch the back-order mess we've got.

They looked around for an existing program but decided we needed something done in-house if we were going to be able to build on existing data instead of starting over. That's when they came to me, and that's why I'm coming to you. How would you like to take the lead on this project?"

Jack had two, opposite, reactions: Yes, this could be interesting and certainly was a welcome opportunity to show Fran just how capable he was; but no, Jack just didn't have a clue as to how to fit this project into his already packed schedule. As usual, yes won over no, and Jack said, "I'd be happy to tackle this one. It sounds like a few modifications of our existing data-bases and a couple of formatted adjustments to some data entry screens should do the trick, don't you think?"

Fran nodded her agreement and gave Jack the names of a cou-ple of people in Accounting and Inventory that he could con-tact for more details. "I'll let the managers in Accounting know that you'll be working on this. My sense from them is that they'd like something as soon as possible, so if you could wrap this up in the next couple of weeks, I think they'll be more than satisfied."

Jack assured Fran that he would have no trouble delivering an easy entry/easy access database in a couple of weeks and made his way back to his workstation. Later that afternoon, he called the key contacts in Accounting and asked them to fax him a list of the features they wanted to include in the software upgrade. Before the end of the day, they had complied with a two-page feature list. "I'll start on this first thing in the morning," Jack thought as he filed the list in a new folder titled "Inventory Management Upgrade."

Fran had decided on Jack for the inventory software upgrade even before her meeting with the accounting managers was over. He was one of her very best programmers and was able to juggle his time so that he made deadlines even though he had a full load of tasks and projects. And, as good as competence and efficiency are, Jack's favorite characteristic, as far as Fran was concerned, was his "can do" attitude. Jack didn't grumble when she gave him new work assignments; he almost always smiled confidently while assuring her that he could fit them in.

From Jack's remarks about the software upgrade, Fran was reassured that the project would go without a hitch. And go it must; Fran not only had a full plate of her own to work on, precluding any time for monitoring or mentoring Jack, but the key decision makers who had asked her to do the project were also key decision makers in selecting the person to go into what she hoped would be her next promotion. "Go, Jack!" was the last real thought Fran gave to the inventory software upgrade project before turning her attention to other things.

Assumptions

Are Jack and Fran headed for trouble? Or do they have every-thing under control? The answer depends on how much actual information Jack gathers about the needs of the inventory soft-ware customers before he begins and/or how many assumptions (read "guesses") he makes about what they want. Like most people who don't want to appear dense when talking to their boss, Jack adopted an expression that said, "I understand what you want and can easily add this new task to my list" instead of asking a lot of potentially dumb questions. Will Jack figure out what he needs to know and ask revealing questions of the right people, or will he fill in the blanks with assumptions?

Guessing isn't necessarily a bad thing. Most people do more guessing than they realize or would admit to. In fact, making assumptions is one of the ways that capable adults get things done quickly. Instead of starting from square one on every new task we're given, we automatically use past information about a person to make predictions about what that person wants and needs. We do the same about work challenges, plugging our ed-ucated guesses in where facts are missing. The more familiar a person or situation appears to us, the more likely we are to make assumptions.

The habit of making assumptions can help us appear smart and can also cause us to outsmart ourselves. Correct assump-tions save the time we'd otherwise spend gathering all the facts. And being able to come up with the best course of action after a brief glimpse at the challenge makes our insight, intelligence, and experience obvious to everyone. But too often, our habit of making assumptions sends us in a direction that ranges from a little to a lot offtrack. We take a sketchy description of a project from our boss, fill in the holes with our best guesses, and start investing our time, resources, and reputation in the production of the wrong outcome. With more facts at our disposal, we'd see how our idea of what the boss wanted is actually different from the desired outcome. But because the assumption habit is so strong, we seldom think to ask the questions that would give us the facts; we've already filled in the information holes with our automatic guesses.

So, big deal! You find out where you guessed wrong while you're solving the problem; you make a little mid-course correction and you still end up ahead. With short-duration or low-priority tasks, that's probably true. But when it comes to projects, making mid-course corrections is more difficult, and the consequences of delays and blown budgets are usually bad enough to warrant avoiding them. The lost time and effort and the frustration and disappointment of prime movers and end users are too big a price to pay. As a general rule, the more of yourself and your company's resources you invest in a project, the more important it is to have a complete and detailed picture of several key factors. "Like what key factors?" I'm glad you asked. Read on!

Facts to Find

Don't start working on a brand new project immediately after meeting with a prime mover. Go to your office, sit down, and collect your thoughts. Dedicate yourself to finding out what you don't know. The seven key factors introduced below will help guide your thinking and, eventually, your information gathering. In later sections of this chapter, we will work on how to personalize the factors to your project and on techniques to exhaustively explore them with prime movers.

1. What's Fueling This Project?

Project work, like most human behavior, is motivated by the desire to get something desirable or remove something unpleasant. Before you ask for a detailed description of the project outcome—that specific result that is expected to yield something desirable and/or terminate something unpleasant—ask questions designed to reveal some of the background events that triggered the decision to invest your time and the other resources in this project. By examining a project's context before you narrow your scope to a specific outcome, you can be creative with your project plans, more responsive to the needs of people who will be using the project outcome, more accurate in prioritizing project activities and, consequently, more efficient and effective. What I mean by "a project's context" are such issues as how long the need has existed, who has been impacted by the problem that will be solved, how others have tried to address the need, and which others are interested in the project's result.

2. How Much Latitude Do You Have in Targeting the Project Outcome and Developing the Project Plan?

Is the prime mover assigning this project or is s/he delegating it? Sometimes prime movers know, or think they know, exactly what they want and how they want you to go about making it appear. They tell and you do. If you're a rookie or if circumstances require that the prime mover make a command decision (that is, time is short, huge financial problems are looming, or the boss has given marching orders on this project), assigning a project makes sense. Other times, prime movers will stop at the "glimmer" stage and look to you to figure out the specifics of a project outcome and plan. The implications of an assignment versus a delegated project are considerable.

Delegated Projects

A delegated project happens when the prime mover says something like, "Shirley, we need a completely updated marketing plan for the new electronic zithers we'll be introducing next quarter. This plan needs all the bells and whistles, but I don't have time to do it. Congratulations, good luck, and have the completed plan on my desk by the end of next month." Having a project delegated to you provides you with enough rope to either hang yourself or shinny up to the next rung on your career ladder. Resources aren't just being invested in the project; they're being invested in a test of your abilities and potential. If you perform well, you'll add to the "can do" reputation that promotions are made of. Of course, you know what will happen if you underperform.

Projects frequently fail because of confusion over what "in charge" means. Too often, reluctant, confused, or just-plain-overworked project leaders divvy up the tasks of a delegated project with the detachment of a person whose future doesn't depend on succeeding. Big mistake! Much like parents who are surprised to find out that their too often ignored child grew up to become an unhappy, unproductive whiner on *Geraldo*, project leaders who treat their role as a nuisance rather than an opportunity usually end up with their heads handed to them when the results are late, halfhearted, or absent entirely. "In charge" means you have a new and important element in your job description: project leader. Treat it as if you love it: Think about it, talk about it, nurture it, pour energy into it, and make it happy. Because hell hath no fury like a project scorned.

Because you shoulder so much responsibility and accountability for the success of a delegated project, you'll need to devote time to finding out exactly what is needed. Avoid the tendency to quickly charge forward to produce what the prime mover thinks is needed. Far too often, prime movers authorize projects and assign outcomes on second- and third-hand information (a supervisor tells a manager who tells a task force that writes a report that the prime mover reads). There may well be a valid need but the project outcome that the prime mover specifies is wrong enough to frustrate already frustrated end users who end up having to implement it. When a project is delegated to you, one of your first and most important tasks is to either confirm that the prime mover's idea of an optimal outcome is accurate or make a good case for modifying it. You'll have to talk to several types of people before you can nail down the best-case outcome, so resign yourself to asking many questions before committing to a specific outcome.

Assigned Projects

Suppose your boss calls you in and says, "Maurice, I need you to develop a marketing plan for me. Here is a complete listing of the people you need to talk to, what you need to ask them, the dates that need to be met and the things that must happen on those dates, the resources you can use, and the exact outcome I'm looking for. I'll expect an update memo every other day and a weekly progress review in my office every Friday. Do you have any questions?" In this case you're not being delegated to;

you're receiving an assignment. Getting an assigned project could mean that (1) the prime mover is a control nut, (2) the company culture is "tell"-oriented rather than consensual, (3) the project specs came down from on high, or (4) you're a rookie who isn't ready to solo but who is getting some supervised flying time. Do a good job and you'll eventually earn the opportunity to receive a delegated project.

The good news about an assigned project would seem to be that you aren't accountable if the result isn't exactly on target. You were just following orders, right? The bad news is that too many prime movers will look for someone to share the blame if the project lays an egg and you'll be high on the list. A word to the wise: If you see a way to improve the outcome of an assigned project, don't keep it to yourself. Use some of the persuasion techniques described in Chapter 6 to help your prime mover and the project succeed.

3. How Big or Small Should This Project Be?

Delegated projects require finding the right point on a range of desired outcomes that runs from "highly efficient and utilitarian" to "something so wonderful that we'll all hop up and down cheering." Of course, that outcome range is typically accompanied with a range of required resources that runs from "peanuts" to "so much money, people, and other stuff that annual bonuses must be postponed."

The project prime mover is the first person you'll want to talk to about his or her outcome and resources expectations. Avoid any habit you or your prime mover might have to shrink options down to specific outcomes and activities. You're objective is to find out minimum and maximum limits on resources and outcomes, not to get an exact and probably misguided specification of what to produce and how to produce it. When you think you've gathered enough information to avoid under- or overengineering the project, end the discussion with reassuring words about gathering more information so that the project will be exactly what everyone wants and needs.

Part of this discussion must involve the project budget. Of course, any outcome is possible, but will it be worth what it takes to produce? Before beginning a project, you need to know if you have a budget and just how big your budget is. The best-case situation is that you know how much the completed project will cost and what you can expect it to cost at specific milestone points throughout. Most mortals are required to operate with considerably less detailed information.

Next, ask end users for their vision of the project outcome. Go to the place they will use the project's result and watch them work on something similar. Find out through observation what the result must do and what it must not do. Accept the risk of asking dumb questions so that you can be sure to get all the facts. You aren't ready to plan your project until you have a clear vision of what the desired outcome should look like, how it should function, who will be using it, and whether the prime mover will support its creation.

4. What Are the Foreseeable Project Politics and Problems?

Many projects must "borrow" budget, people, and other resources to get off the ground. Does the mere mention of the prime mover's name give you the juice to get what you want when you want it from people who are glad to give? Or must you "tin cup" resources from reluctant or downright resistant sources? By tactfully gathering information about the project's level of support, you can usually make very educated guesses about the project's ability to survive until completion. As a general rule, longer-duration, higher-cost projects need much more widespread and enthusiastic support than shorter, cheaper projects. If you receive a project delegation or assignment with a narrow base of support, you would be wise to either drum up interest from others or prepare yourself for the possibility of mid-project shelving.

If you aren't the technical expert for this project, locate and spend time with the most knowledgeable person you can. Ask about their experiences and about any tough technical problems they ran into. As you go through the planning and execution stages of the task, you are bound to run into problems, but by anticipating as many as possible, you can minimize their impact on your schedule and your results.

5. *What Is the Project Priority?*

You probably had plenty to do before you were asked to do this project, so now you've ventured into the increasingly familiar territory called "Overload." The natural reaction may be to simply suck it up—to get to work earlier and/or leave later. Sometimes that's the best thing to do. But other times, you owe it to yourself and to the kids who are about to call you "Uncle Daddy" or "Aunt Mommy" to have a chat with the prime mover. Specifically, ask for guidance in reprioritizing your schedule. What deadlines can be moved back? Should you off-load one of your tasks to someone else or shelve it? What proportion of your time should be devoted to the new project?

Certainly, there are times when you can or must shift into overdrive to get everything done, but sometimes overdrive isn't warranted or sufficient. Before burning yourself out or blowing a deadline, ask for some input.

6. *What Update and Documentation Expectation Does the Prime Mover Have?*

The prime mover giveth and the prime mover can taketh away. Of the several reasons for keeping a prime mover updated, project security may be one of the most important. If your project requires several weeks to complete, you need to be updating/reselling the prime mover on its merits if you want to avoid being shelved in favor of a newer, shinier project.

If the participants in a project are going to change throughout or if you expect questions about the amount of resources required by a project, plan on documenting the what, why, how, and how much of each project element. The prime mover can give you advice on how much documentation will be enough.

7. *What Is the Deadline?*

"Deadline" is an excellent way to express that point in time beyond which the results of your project and some part of your hoped-for annual bonus will pass on to the netherworld. Find out the prime mover's desired delivery and the definitely dead dates. Then add up all the days between then and now, factor in the priority and resource information you gathered earlier, and make a rough estimate of how realistic the deadline is. After you recover from the spasm of nervous laughter, select the aspect of the project you'd prefer to negotiate: more time, more help, or a more realistic outcome. But whatever you do, resist the temptation to skip any more fact finding or planning in favor of producing a result. An overdeveloped sense of urgency has sent many well-intentioned project leaders in directions that are beset with anticipatable problems, reinvented wheels, and half-right outcomes.

Although the seven factors described above aren't carved in granite, they can provide you with a foundation of information upon which project planning can be done. As you read through them, you may come up with additional specific factors to probe or you could develop a curiosity itch that can be scratched only by asking spontaneous, free-form questions. In either case, remember that information is power and you'll need all the power you can lay your hands on to take most projects home.

Time Out for Thinking

With your list of project planning topics in hand but before you actually go out and gather information, it's time to do something few people do enough of: Think. Resist "can do, go get 'em" habits; it's time to make sure that you work smart. Make use of your curiosity to see around the corners of your project's path. Use your experience, your intuition, and your paranoia to anticipate the budget and schedule angels and gremlins. Get in touch with your ignorance and with the assumptions you've made but can't strongly support. Add your project-specific thoughts, concerns, issues, and/or ideas to each of the seven project factors. Next, add the thinking power of someone who is knowledgeable and insightful. Discuss your expanded list with them and ask for their reactions and suggestions; then sit very quietly and listen. Take notes. Only when they run out of gas should you respond and/or react. If need be, clarify and/or confirm what they've said, but always thank them profusely. This may feel like wasting time but thinking is actually one of the activities that distinguishes humans from monkeys. You're well on your way to knowing what to ask about. Now you can work on how to dig out the information you need to effectively lead the project.

Probe for Information

For several reasons, asking questions isn't a very good way to get information. Here are two: People won't tell you all you need to know, and you won't listen very well to what they say. It's no wonder that poor communication is at the bottom of so much misery (number-one complaint in divorce) and inefficiency (ponder the root cause of meltdowns you've had at work). Let me explain.

Questions are spontaneous. You look at your list of key factors and see "Budget." So you ask, "How much money do we have set aside to support this project?" Your prime mover says, "There isn't any funding set aside for this project at the present time." Perplexed, you ask, "When will we get some funding?" The prime mover says, "I don't know." Even more puzzled by this no-fund project, you blurt, "Then don't you think we should put this on hold until some funding appears?" The prime mover pauses as she examines a sharp-looking letter opener. "No." That uncomfortable feeling in your mouth is your foot.

Of course, most people you talk to will be more forthcoming, but occasionally you'll try to interview someone who is not trying to help. And more often, you'll interview people who have so much on their own plate that their priority for your fact-finding meeting is that you finish as quickly as possible. They'll give you the information that you ask for, but they won't do your thinking for you. If your spontaneous questions aren't clear, comprehensive, and insightful, their answers won't be either.

Most people have a little voice inside their head that talks to them (some folks have two or more). We tend to think of that voice as the real "us," and given any kind of excuse we listen to the inner "us" rather than the outer anyone. When you're fact finding with questions, you'll be listening to your inner voice make up and rehearse the next question while the other person in the room is answering the last one. Of course, your eyes and ears will be pointed at the other person, but your attention will be focused on yourself; this is an extremely common habit that accounts for many, many mistakes. We half hear someone's response to an ill-planned question and, rather than request clarification, we avoid embarrassment by filling in the void with an assumption.

Anchor your fact finding around planned questions, known as probes. Develop some probes for each key topic, and supplement them with follow-up questions. So how, you're probably thinking, do you "specially design" questions?

Let's start by considering two major types of probes: open and closed. An open probe is a planned question that cannot be answered with either yes or no. For example:

"Tell me about the intended end users."

"How is this report going to be used?"

"Describe the problems you ran into when you worked on a similar task."

Open probes are useful because they:

1. Give you an overview of information when you are ignorant about a topic (e.g., "I'm new to the marketing department's function, so it would be very helpful if you described your normal process for developing an ad campaign").

2. Reveal opinions, assumptions, and biases before you dig a hole with opinions of your own (e.g., "I've been given an overview of the Department of Labor's allegations that we have a glass ceiling here, but before I begin developing a diversity program for the entire company, I'd like your take on the scope and breadth of gender discrimination here").

3. Allow the speaker to hear his/her favorite sound for a while. Depending on the person you're interviewing, open probes can either reveal a mother lode of information or open

the floodgates of blah-blah. In either case, you'll be building rapport and, in the event of blah-blah, you can reel in and nail down the talker with some closed probes.

A closed probe is a planned question that can be answered only with yes or no. For example:

> "As I understand it, the end users will be any store personnel who have occasion to operate the cash registers. Is that correct?"

> "Would I be accurate in saying that this report will be used to support the purchase of new computer equipment?"

> "Would you say that the biggest problem you ran into when you worked on the widget project was getting an acceptable throughput rate?"

The most important functions of closed probes are to clarify and/or confirm. As the person you're speaking with answers your open probes, you'll want to clarify and confirm specific facts for yourself or, in some cases, for the other person (e.g., "It sounds like you're leaning toward a fourth-quarter rollout of the new product. Is that correct?). It is answers to closed probes that let you build plans and set schedules. But they also rein in blah-blah artists and focus fuzzy thinkers. And they severely limit the wiggle room some overly political or just-plain-nervous people try to build into their answers.

Probe Pyramids

The label "probe pyramid" is a word picture of the way probes can be used for maximum effect. Most interviews will involve several probe pyramids that correspond to the topics you want to explore. At the base or beginning of a pyramid (see Figure 1-1), you'll ask a broad open probe designed to elicit a big-picture overview. The answer allows you to catalogue and prioritize key topic issues and helps you pursue more specific topic information comprehensively and according to its priority. After one or

Figure 1-1. Probe pyramids.

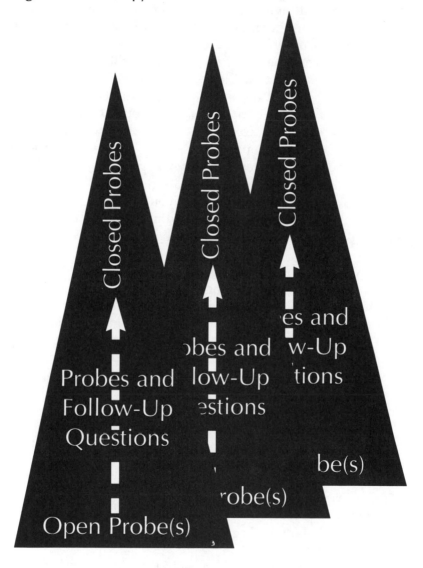

more broad open probes about the topic, you'll have enough information to follow up with informed questions and, eventually, finish the pyramid and the topic with one or more information-confirming or commitment-sealing closed probes. At this point, you can smoothly jump to the next pyramid by asking a broad open probe designed to open up the new topic.

Effective fact-finding interviews feel and sound natural. As such, the probes you ask should be prepared and rehearsed in your spoken voice rather than on paper. Writing probes word for word is too slow and will make you sound like a windup interviewer. With the list of topics you want to explore in hand, rehearse open probes that "open up" each topic. Using phrases like "Tell me about. . . ," Describe. . . ," and "Bring me up to speed on . . . ," rehearse open probes until you're comfortable with them and are confident that they'll produce the desired effect.

Next, list words that will remind you about the more-specific information you need to gather while you're in each key topic area. As before, rehearse open probes until you're comfortable and confident.

Finally, write closed probe cues on your list for each fact you must confirm before moving out of a particular pyramid. Rather than rehearse Joe Friday's part in *Dragnet*, however, use the following formula: State the "fact" you're trying to clarify or confirm followed by "Is that correct?" For example, as you look at "Budget Commitment—March" on your list, you are reminded to ask, "We will have a budget of $40,000 committed to this project by the first of March. Is that correct?". This will save on prep time and get you a straight answer every time.

Using probe pyramids brings you four valuable benefits. They:

1. Make sure that you cover all the important information.
2. Confirm specific key facts.
3. Help the person being interviewed by developing each topic gradually and separately (as opposed to "shotgunning" unrelated topics).
4. Make your notes and memory of the interview better organized.

As you can see from Figure 1-1, not all questions in a pyramid are planned; they can't be. In topic areas where your advance information is limited, the best you can hope for is to follow the initial open probes with follow-up questions. As you uncover more information, you'll either ask open-ended questions (to keep the person talking) or closed-ended questions (to confirm, clarify, or get a commitment). But in most cases, you can plan one or more open probes that will point the interviewee in the right direction and one or more closed probes to confirm information you'll need to start the project.

Here are some examples of three pyramid probe sets designed to explore and confirm the topics of:

1. Problems with the status quo
2. User-friendliness
3. User requirements

Pyramid Set A

"Tell me about the end users' problems with their present inventory system and why they came to us to help solve them." [*Open*]

"What have they tried to do in the past to solve these problems?" [*Open*]

"If I understand you correctly, the reason they couldn't use a simple extension of Orgomax Database is because it didn't have the updating capabilities that they require. Is that correct?" [*Closed*]

Pyramid Set B

"What are their expectations, if any, regarding user-friendliness?" [*Open*]

"Then they want a program that allows them to add, change, and delete inventory data without any user training. Is that correct?" [*Closed*]

Pyramid Set C

"Tell me about their size and speed requirements." [*Open*]

"Then we need to supply them with a desktop unit that holds a minimum of 500 megabytes and operates at 60 megahertz or more. Is that correct?" [*Closed*]

Fact Finding and Probe Use in the Real World

Let's consider how probes can be applied to your "real world" projects. When your boss or some other prime mover asks you to manage a new project, you won't have enough time to listen and figure out the probes that will fill in your ignorance gaps. You can certainly ask questions from each of the seven key factors we considered earlier and from any others you come up with yourself, but even then, you'll probably leave the meeting with less than you need to proceed. So, make a point to set a second meeting with the prime mover as soon as possible to go in and probe. In the meantime, work through each factor and decide what you know and what you need to know. Using your key factor musings as a base, prepare a list of words or phrases that will cue you to ask the probes you've been rehearsing. Of course, your list of cue words/phrases should be organized as probe pyramids, with an open probe cue to launch each key factor and closed probe cues to remind you to nail down specific facts:

> "Then they will want written documentation. Is that correct?"
>
> "It would be possible to wait until the 15th to start. Is that correct?"
>
> "They will identify someone to provide me with information about their existing procedures. Is that correct?"

There are three truths about probing:

1. It takes more time in the beginning, but saves considerable time and trouble later on.
2. It frequently forces prime movers and end users to clarify their thinking and expectations.
3. It makes you look good on the front end ("Isn't s/he detailed and professional in how s/he really lines out a project before s/he starts?"), during the probing ("The way s/he anticipated that problem: It's as if s/he could see around corners!), and when you finish ("This is great! We got exactly what we wanted and right on schedule too!).

Chapter 2
Getting Help From Other People

Doing depends upon learning, not learning upon doing.
[Therefore,] learning must precede practice.

—Jerusalem Talmud, Pesahim

I'll learn him or kill him.

—Mark Twain, *Life on the Mississippi*

Jack knew that he couldn't finish the inventory software project without help. The time he'd lost racing off in wrong directions put him on a schedule that was somewhere between tight and impossible. To deliver an acceptable software upgrade in time,

Jack would need a couple of hours a day from three or four people. Running through his "file" of people owing favors, Jack quickly compiled a hit list.

Looking for a quick yes, Jack called Jennifer. She owed Jack for work he had helped her with last month and she was eager to even the score. Jennifer listened attentively as Jack described the project and actually interrupted Jack with her offer to help. Twenty minutes later, however, Jennifer was still confused about how to do some of the tasks Jack was trying to delegate to her. Jennifer was neither stupid nor a slow starter, but she was very unfamiliar with key tasks in Jack's project and would require a lot of instruction before she was up to speed.

Jack's next call went to Raul, a potential project hero. About three months ago, Jack had attended a technical training program where he met Raul and became very impressed by his knowledge, insight, and sense of humor. Even in areas that were completely new, Raul had an intuitive understanding that Jack wanted working on his inventory software upgrade project. Connecting with Raul required a morning of phone tag, but once Jack made contact, Raul cordially remembered Jack and expressed sincere interest in helping. But before Jack could explain what he needed, Raul had to take a call from a client and handle some urgent tasks. Promising to get back tomorrow or the next day, Raul disappeared into the phone system in a cloud of dust and a hearty "Hiho, Silver."

Before calling Milton, Jack decided to dose himself with Tylenol; better to have the remedy already working in the bloodstream than to spend ten painful minutes listening to Mr. Whiny Voice without benefit of medication. Under normal circumstances, Jack would find a way to complete the project without Milton, but with his back to the wall, tapping into Milton's ever-present free time was the shortcut Jack needed. Milton might be a royal pain to be around, but he had an uncanny ability to survive rightsizing and avoid the overload condition that everyone else worked under. So Jack endured five minutes of Milton's various illnesses, seven minutes of carping about office politics, and another five of how busy he was with his own work. And, having paid the price of polite listening, Jack was rewarded with Milton's grudging agreement to help.

Just as Jack was straining his brain to find one more name on his helper hit list, a strange and wonderful thing happened. Wanda appeared in his doorway with a smile and an offer. Her boss was vitally interested in the software upgrade project and wanted Wanda to give Jack a hand. It took only a couple of minutes of talk for Jack to discover that Wanda was fully briefed and very capable. She brought an understanding of the end users' needs as well as strong technical skills and equally strong enthusiasm. As he listened, Jack made some tentative calculations and concluded that, with help from Wanda and his other three recruits, the upgrade project could be brought in on time. Poor deluded Jack!

With the exception of Wanda, Jack's helpers can easily turn out to be more trouble than they are worth. Jennifer wants to help but is ignorant enough about the project to require almost constant support from Jack. Raul is capable but very unlikely to give Jack's project enough time. Most talented and enthusiastic workers have schedules filled with their own job requirements and promises of help to others. Getting their attention and assistance often requires either authority or a long-standing relationship. Jack should have saved the Tylenol for a better purpose than curing Milton-induced pain. Although he is a warm body, Milton's overworked attitude and underdeveloped ability has "high risk" written all over it.

So what's a person to do? Almost by definition, project leaders do not have the position power to pick and choose the best possible project collaborators or to wave the motivational authority wand over their heads. Hat in hand, you will find yourself soliciting help from people who may or may not know enough to add value to your project (known as the "can't do" crowd) and from people who have the right, and sometimes the clear directive, to say no (the "won't do" crowd). Let's use all of the possible combinations of "can't" and "won't" to take a closer look at what we must do to get collaborators on board our project and how we must lead them in order to help them be all that they can be (see Figure 2-1).

Jennifer is willing to help, but she isn't able to add value without a big investment of time from Jack. By listening to her questions and asking a few of his own, Jack discovered that Jennifer had more energy than expertise. Left to her own devices, Jennifer would spin her wheels until she dug a hole big enough to deposit any and all motivation she had for the project. Jack needs to either find a training program that can teach her what she needs to know, invest time and effort in monitoring a detailed delegation of project tasks, or find someone who is more able.

Raul is able, but probably isn't willing to jettison some of his job duties and/or promises of help to others. In the final mix, Raul is very likely to disappoint Jack just when Raul's help would make the difference. Jack needs to either persuade Raul

Figure 2-1. Four categories of project candidates.

COMPETENCE

	High	Low
High	Willing and Able	Willing but Not Able
Low	Not Willing But Able	Not Willing and Not Able

PRIORITY

directly, persuade Raul's boss, or look for someone who is more willing.

Milton is neither willing nor able. If Jack relies on Milton to move any part of the project forward, laying in a store of Tylenol would be wise. Milton is very likely to add the insult of excuses to the injury of a compromised schedule. Jack can try to arrange some training for Milton, but the prognosis for improvement is bleak. Or Jack can steal some more time away from his family and coach Milton directly. With close-contact coaching, the prognosis for improvement is better than it would be if Jack relied on training, but even with coaching, the return on an investment like this is almost always marginal. Jack's wisest move would be to lose the Rolodex card with Milton's number on it.

Wanda (or as Jack calls her, Wandaful) is ready, willing, and able. Jack needs to brief her on the project plan, confirm milestone assignments, and get out of her way.

As you can see from the four extremes above, how you go about getting help from others should be driven by your assessment of each individual's ability to perform and the priority—time and urgency—they give to the project. A how-to discussion of the four approaches toward securing help—delegation, assignment, persuasion, and coaching/training—consume the remainder of this chapter.

Delegating Project Tasks to the Willing but Semi-Able

Perhaps because the practice of cavalierly dumping the responsibility of producing poorly explained outcomes into the laps of direct reports who cannot say no has been called *delegation* by so many overtaxed bosses, too many people seem to think that delegation is just a nice synonym for *dump*. Real delegation isn't about reporting relationships or pruning necessary busywork from an overloaded in-box. It is about leveraging a person's interest and enthusiasm so that s/he can learn a new competency.

Many attempts at project delegation fail because tasks and outcomes are delegated without a detailed discussion of the facts that have been found earlier and/or possible resources that could be called upon. From the delegator/project leader's perspective, one of the big, ugly, and unfamiliar project milestones that was busy nestling on his or her shoulders has been successfully transplanted to someone else's back. From the project participant/delegatee's standpoint, new work from a nonboss has taken up residence at the bottom of his or her priority stack and will be procrastinated accordingly. It is only human nature that a project participant would put the tasks and outcomes that count at evaluation time ahead of unfamiliar work that has been delegated by someone who can't impact his/her job rating or salary. Without some special care by the project leader, a delegated project milestone has a very high likelihood of turning into a bottleneck.

Delegating a project milestone to someone who is willing but not skilled in the tasks that are required is like training, because new skills must be developed. But delegation requires more of the participant/learner than training does. Training success depends on a skillful instructor, a carefully designed program, and a willing, attentive learner. Successful delegation relies on detailed information from the delegator and enough curiosity and motivation on the individual's part to figure out what s/he must learn and do to produce the targeted result.

Before we address the practical issues of effective delegation, let's be entirely clear about the consequences of poorly and well-done delegation. Poor planning on the delegator's part usually guarantees confusion, resistance, missed deadlines, and marginal results. The delegator puts his project in jeopardy and loses any goodwill s/he had with the dazed delegatee/project participant. You lose, the participant loses, the project loses, and your organization loses. It doesn't have to be that way. If you invest some time in planning and monitoring your delegations, you can directly connect with the good side of the force. The payoffs of effective delegation go well beyond a successful project; effective delegation expands competency, builds motivation, enhances job mobility, and saves the resources that would be spent on less self-directed, more costly development alternatives, such as classroom training. As a project leader who delegates, you're not only getting your project done, you're strengthening your company and saving it money.

Adequate delegation of a project milestone begins with a comprehensive, two-way meeting. The objective of the meeting is to fully explain the milestone and likely ways to produce it. With a motivated collaborator, you should be able to provide enough information and guidance so that s/he can independently learn enough to produce the valuable results your project requires both on schedule and within budget. The key agenda items for this meeting are explained below:

1. *Project milestone result specifications.* When you tell people what to do, you strip them of outcome ownership and task motivation. When you tell people the outcome you need and discuss their thoughts on how to produce those results, you promote them to partner as you fuel the flames of ownership and interest. Of course, a delegated task isn't going to be done with maximum efficiency because the delegatee is learning what to do and how to do it, but you may get some creative wrinkles that a routine approach to the task wouldn't reveal. And if you describe the required result with enough attention to detail, you'll end up with the result you want.

2. *Rationale for the project.* There are two reasons to spend some time discussing the delegated work in terms of the big picture. First, the fresh eyes of a novice might see something that others (like you) have missed: something that allows the result to be completed more efficiently or that allows for an improved result. Breakthroughs do happen when rookies teach themselves how to produce a result. Second, work becomes drudgery when people aren't aware of how their efforts contribute to the whole. When you take the time to talk about how the project results will benefit the company, your clients, and your coworkers, you empower the delegatee.

3. *Milestone and project deadline(s).* Give some thought to when you want the result and when you need it. Most new work takes longer than the rookie thinks it will, so you may want to build in a fudge factor if the result being delegated is a potential schedule buster. On the other hand, if you build in too much "comfort zone" between the deadline and the "terminally dead" deadline, you may get what you want only to alienate the delegatee when s/he finds out that frantic work saved your mental health instead of the project schedule.

4. *Available resources for project work.* Because a delegated task is outside the scope of regularly assigned work, the delegatee might need additional tools, access or some other resource that isn't readily available or well known. It's your job to use your authority (or your prime mover's authority) to get the resources your delegatee will need to succeed. Because the delegatee will be learning about the task right up to the minute s/he finishes it, encourage her/him to ask for resources whenever the need arises.

5. *Monitoring the participant's work.* Too many delegations— usually the disasters—have one monitoring point, which occurs on the deadline. Project leaders who are too busy to monitor and project participants who don't want an audience as they struggle to learn new skills can unwittingly conspire to stay in the dark until the fireball of a blown deadline illuminates their mutual meltdown.

Figuring out how much monitoring is enough requires an effort on both parts to find the comfort zone between meltdown worries on one end and micromanagement mania on the other. The less a delegatee knows about producing a result, the more monitoring (at the beginning, middle, and end) you should schedule. And the more competition there is for the delegatee's time and attention, the more a wise project leader monitors to be sure that the delegated milestone hasn't sunk to the bottom of the priority pool.

6. *Advice from the project leader.* Go light on the advice. Even though you have much more project background information than anyone else, the more a project leader suggests, the less pride a delegatee can have in the result. If you know some likely potholes or wrong turns, point them out. But as soon as you find yourself sounding like Yoda, the intergalactic oracle from the *Starwars Trilogy,* consider shutting up.

7. *The priority of project work.* Now that the delegatee knows what you want, it's going to be important to find out where project work fits into the schedule of other tasks and outcomes. Will work on your project milestone get as much time and energy as his or her most important work or will it fill in dead spots during the day? You'll want to know whether the delegatee consistently plans and schedules his or her work or, like so many people, tends to forsake planning in favor of reacting to fast-breaking emergencies. If you get even a hint that the delegatee is either a firefighter who runs from blaze to blaze or an overpromiser who never learned how to just say no, beware. Revisit paragraph 5, "Monitoring . . . ," and set some hard and fast milestone dates to review progress. You would also be wise to chat with the delegatee's boss to firm up your claim on his or her direct report's time and efforts. Far too many projects go down the tube because overpromisers or time-mismanaged people pull out at the last moment. Nail 'em down!

8. *Making commitments to each other.* Professional persuaders consider all the talking that precedes a firm commitment "happy talk," that agreeable posturing people do before they are asked to lock into an agreement that involves consequences. As a project leader, you are asking a member of someone else's team to spend some time and energy playing in your special event. In this age of doing more with less and fewer, the act of borrowing

another team's fullback to play in your All-Star game requires, at a minimum, asking, "Will you talk to me before you let anyone drag you off the project?"

Assigning Project Work to the Willing and Able

Unlike delegation, which is a learning process, assignment is simply telling a ready, willing, and able person what outcome you need and when you need it. Even though the people to whom you assign project work are (1) familiar with the tasks and outcomes, (2) quite capable of producing the project milestones you need, and (3) motivated to complete the work on schedule, the safest way to assign project work is to treat it like delegation, following each of the steps listed above. The worst that could happen is you'll be telling the person things s/he already knows. But when you compare that minor inefficiency with reducing any chance of a project meltdown caused by a faulty assumption, the right choice is obvious.

Persuading the Able but Unwilling

Project work is frequently above and beyond the call of duty. With an already full plate, most potential project participants are going to resist taking on any more work if they can. This is especially true of people who are more skillful and, therefore, in demand. For these reasons, convincing an already busy person to deprioritize part of his or her job in order to work on your project task will require a strong understanding of motivation, a ready command of persuasion skills, and an investment of time spent persuading them. And in many cases, you'll have to influence the person's boss before you can get your potential participant's final OK. Finding and reeling in these big fish start during fact finding.

Earning the Right to Persuade

The fact-finding phase of your project involves more than gathering the information necessary to plan a high-yield project.

While you are harvesting information, you will also be trolling for the high-potential participants who can make your project go faster, easier, and better than a cross section of average participants could. So, as you talk to the prime mover, stakeholders, technical experts, and all other fact-finding targets, be sure to ask for the names of people who have a particular talent or a results track record: "Whom do you know who has experience doing X?" When you get names, put them on your fact-finding hit list. You will want to interview them as part of your fact finding for the project, but you'll also be evaluating and influencing them.

Projecting the qualities of focus and efficiency are always important, but they take on special value when you're talking with people you may want to persuade to join your project. If they're good, they are already plenty busy, so take pains to demonstrate your respect for their time. Arrive at your fact-finding meeting(s) on time or a little early and come with preplanned questions. Don't open the interview with small talk; instead, cut to the chase. For example:

> *Project Manager:* I appreciate the thirty minutes you've given me today, and I want to make the very best use of them. I've got four topics—A, B, C, and D—I'd like to ask questions about. Are there any other issues we should explore that you believe would be important to the project?

In addition to gathering information, your objective during a fact-finding interview is to make potentially valuable collaborators want to work with you. By demonstrating focus, clarity, respect, and a results orientation every time you talk to potential project heros, they'll believe that you have thought about the project and will approach it in an organized, planned way. By taking care to treat first-round draft picks with an extra measure of respect, you give them what they believe they have already earned by virtue of their competence and hard work. And emphasizing your results orientation, you communicate that you and your project are not going to squander today's most valuable resource: time.

Toward the end of fact finding but before you've obtained commitments from all your project participants, you will have removed the hopelessly busy and the marginally helpful from your list of potential collaborators. You have earned the right to ask for help from those who remain by virtue of the interest, focus, and respect you communicated as you interviewed them. But in most cases, it will take more than a positive regard for you and the value of your project to get the commitment to participate that you'll need. You've got to sell them on the idea of joining your project, and that means you need to know a little more about human nature and the psychology of persuasion. For that, let's turn to an allegory called "Bernie and the Bird."

Human Nature and the Tactics of Persuasion: "Bernie and the Bird"

Persuasion isn't very complicated or hard to master; if it were, we wouldn't have so many politicians, car salespeople, or lobbyists. In fact, the bedrock ideas of persuasion can be fully appreciated by getting to know Bernie and the Bird, an invisible and inseparable pair who reside in all of us.

Bernie is a big, not very verbal creature whose thoughts, interests, and behavior center around what feels good and what

feels bad. He is as uncomplicated as he is single-minded. His behavior at work and at home reflects his desire to move toward things that feel good and away from things that feel bad. In conversations, Bernie daydreams about pleasant things or worries about unpleasant things until the topic turns to real ways to acquire what feels good or avoid what might feel bad. Then you may hear him ask some questions and you'll see him listening attentively.

Perched on Bernie's shoulder is the Bird. Unlike Bernie, the Bird has a large vocabulary, filled with abstract concepts, metaphors, similes, and the other constructs that exist beyond the literal world. With so many words and ideas at his command, the Bird loves to talk. When you propose a course of action or give feedback to Bernie and the Bird, the Bird will analyze, compare, contrast, debate, discuss, evaluate, and intellectualize with all the energy and interest he can summon. While the Bird chatters on, Bernie is usually silent. Eventually, the Bird will turn his beak toward Bernie's ear and, in an attempt to elicit some action, will cluck up a storm of plans, observations, and suggestions. For Bernie, the Bird's energetic talking is little more than background noise. If the Bird hits on something that Bernie perceives as feel-good/feel-bad, he'll listen, but the bulk of the Bird's core dump won't make it past Bernie's ear and into his head.

When the Bird isn't responding to someone else, he can usually be heard generating logical explanations for Bernie's good-seeking/bad-avoiding behavior. Though the Bird isn't in the driver's seat when it comes to Bernie's actions (and his own actions too, since the Bird is always perched on Bernie's shoulder), nothing prevents him from developing a logical-sounding rationale for Bernie's behavior. In almost every situation, the Bird can quickly and effectively create a verbal disguise of reasonableness and productivity that cloaks Bernie's true and fairly simple motivation.

Modern behaviorism revealed the Bernie in human behavior when the processes of positive and negative reinforcement were documented. Rejecting the huge dependence that psychoanalysis places on verbal self-description and the elusive concept known as the "mind," pioneers like B. F. Skinner and thousands of other behavioral scientists took the Bird out of the driver's seat of motivation and looked more closely at Bernie's role. But with decades of research and tens of thousands of scientific studies and countless practical examples to the contrary, most untrained people still let their Bird try to influence someone else's Bird. The persuader's Bird core-dumps literal facts and details, which the persuadee Bird listens to, analyzes, and discusses. As this factual clucking goes back and forth, very little real persuading goes on until and unless the persuader Bird stumbles onto something that sounds like a feel-good or feel-bad to the other person's Bernie.

What can we learn about persuasion from Bernie and the Bird? If you want someone to join your project, tell their Bernie about some aspect of project participation that will feel good or, if you must, tell their Bernie about the feel-bad they can expect if they don't participate. Of course, to do that, you must find out what the individual feel-goods and feel-bads are. During fact finding, ask probes that reveal what their Bernie likes:

"What kinds of work do you like best?"

"How do you feel about getting a chance to preview some new software?"

"Don't you think exposure to the senior management team would improve your chances of being recognized?"

and dislikes:

"Does last-minute, reactive work frustrate you?"

"Do you ever feel you're just repeating the same tasks over and over again?"

When you identify a key player's feel-good/feel-bad issues, practice talking about them between conversations. Think about and practice how you can connect their feel-goods to participation in the project. Work on answering the question, "How can I tell this person's Bernie how s/he'll get this feel-good (or avoid this feel-bad) from working on my project?" And while you rehearse, dream up some questions you can ask Bernie to confirm that he understood your key points and get him actively involved in talking about how the project would make him feel good or allow him to avoid something that feels bad. To persuade someone, you need to think the way their Bernie thinks. When you feel ready to persuade Bernie, begin the conversation with a feel-good windup. For example, if you were going to persuade the highly capable but overbooked Raul to find time in his busy schedule to work on your project, you might start a conversation with him like this:

> *Project Manager:* Raul, during the conversations we've been having, I've learned a lot about you and I've come to value your ability and enthusiasm. I'm putting together a project that I think could really benefit from your participation and that you would enjoy working on. Let me take a minute to explain. We're going to develop an upgrade of inventory software that will be used throughout the company. Your role would be to design the user interface and supervise the coding work that others will be doing. Because of your talent and experience in designing user-friendly computer functions and your excellent communication skills, you're a natural for the project. And that role includes exposure to senior management that should help you achieve the career goals we've talked about. When they see how well you organize and motivate the coding clerks, I have to believe you'll get in line for a supervisory position."

Once you've warmed up Raul's Bernie, use a temperature-taking/involvement question:

> *Project Manager:* Doesn't this sound like a great way to improve our inventory process while you further your career goals?

If Raul's Bernie sounds interested—that is, he asks about the feel-good—keep going down your list of feel-goods and probes until you sense that he's ready to make a commitment. But if he hesitates or resists your proposed change, don't let your Bird start talking (he'll want to). And don't argue with Bernie (he'll move away from you if you make him feel bad). Instead, smile and ask him to tell you about his feel-bad concern. Listen attentively as Raul's Bernie describes something about your proposition that he thinks will end up making him feel bad, or worse than if he kept going on his current course.

> *Raul:*   Look, Jack. I appreciate your kind words and your interest in helping me move my career forward. But I am simply swamped. I've got enough work on my desk now to last me to the end of the year, and it doesn't look as if anything is going to let up. The project sounds interesting, but I just don't have the time!

Remember that while Raul's Bernie is telling you about a potential feel-bad ("If I don't get my existing work done on time, people will be upset with me because I failed them!"), he is expecting you to argue with him when he's done. If you say anything that smells of arguing, Bernie will start moving away. Raul will still be sitting there, but his Bernie will tune you out. So when Raul's Bernie is done, the first words out of your mouth should demonstrate understanding, concern, and a desire to help without bailing out on your persuasion attempt. Restate the concern or reservation, but in terms of a mere problem, not an absolute showstopper. Then ask if you could help change things; your purpose here, of course, is to reduce his Bernie's potential for feeling bad or make it go away entirely.

> *Project Manager:*   I can certainly understand that without some serious adjustments to your heavy workload, it would be impossible for you to commit yourself to this project. It's just a shame to miss out on something that could be so helpful to both of us. I know the project would benefit from your involvement, and it provides such a great showcase for your supervisory potential. It would be a shame to miss out on supervisory position openings because management didn't know just how good you'd be. If it's OK with you, I think there

may be some value in exploring some of our options. Would you feel comfortable if we had a conversation with your boss about this project? If he knew more about it and the impact it will have on the company, he might be willing to adjust your schedule so you can make a contribution.

If Raul's Bernie seems willing to let you help overcome his reservations, ask questions to prepare you for the next Bernie (the boss's Bernie) you'll be talking to.

> *Project Manager:* Tell me a little about your boss. What would his chief concerns (feel-bads) be about adjusting your schedule so you could participate. And what do you think we could emphasize to let him know that this is a really good idea (feel-good)?

If Raul's Bernie resists your idea—for example, he says his boss would go ballistic if you tried to borrow one of his best people—your best bet is to back off and regroup. At this point, if you press most Bernies, they will begin to move away. You're better off ending the conversation with a request for another meeting later and a feel-good teaser.

> *Project Manager:* You know your boss a lot better than I do, and the last thing I want to do is cause you any trouble. What if I start looking for someone else who can do the design and supervision work we talked about and, at the same time, try to figure out how you could work on this project. If I can come up with a bright idea, I'll give you a call. Who knows—there might be a way to get you involved that we just haven't thought of yet. What do you say?

At the very least, Raul is going to let you think about him. And there's a good chance he'll be thinking about you and the project. So, assuming Raul doesn't call you back with good news, you can do one of the following:

1. Find things to add to Raul's feel good/feel bad list that will start his Bernie moving in your direction.
2. Dream up some boss-specific feel-good/feel-bad ammunition you can discuss with Raul.
3. Invest enough time building your relationship with this particular Bernie so that working with you feels good enough to attract a commitment.
4. Search out a Raul replacement.

If, after persuading his Bernie, Raul seems open to joining your project, ask for his commitment.

> *Project Manager:*   That's great, Raul. Then I can look forward to your getting involved in some of the project planning discussions and in the design and supervision activities we've already discussed?

If it's the Bernie of Raul's boss that you're convincing, ask for his commitment.

> *Project Manager:*   Then you're willing to help Raul make time in his schedule to devote eight or nine hours a week to this project?

Remember, until and unless they make a commitment to your project, potential collaborators are likely to bail out and usually at the worst possible time—when they're needed.

Persuasion won't get every key collaborator you pursue for your project, but you can improve your chances by building a reputation of focus, efficiency, concern, understanding, and sensitivity. Sometimes the best persuasion happens when you respect another person's feel-bad concerns enough to back off even when you want him or her. When people trust that you are interested in providing them with feel-goods and unwilling to make them endure feel-bads, they will gravitate toward you whenever possible.

Coaching or Training the Unwilling and Semi-Able

Before you decide to coach a participant who, for whatever reason, neither wants to work on your project nor is skilled in the work activities called for by your project, carefully consider finding someone else. Without your consistent support and guidance, reluctant incompetents are almost sure to give you more and worse mistakes than any other combination of willing and able. As a result, you'll end up teaching them the skills required to participate in the project (which is always more time-consuming than doing it yourself) while you try to lure their Bernie toward you and the project work. Simply put, coaching is a huge investment of time and energy that you'll divert from your normal work and from the project. Unless you can anticipate some future return on this investment or you have no other choice, you're better off not making it.

The first rule of coaching is to have some fun. If you and your reluctant incompetent don't want to be involved in learning a new skill, it won't take your student long to find a way out. Psych yourself into being patient. Show interest in the individual and take some time to reveal yourself a little. Decide to view the inevitable mistakes as learning opportunities instead of setbacks. In short, develop a relationship that causes the student to want to please you and to want to work with you in the future as well as the present.

Give the student the same information you'd give someone accepting a delegation. One common reason why people resist new work assignments centers on a concern that their ignorance will be revealed. No one likes to appear ignorant, particularly when their job competence may be on the line. Be sensitive to the likelihood that you'll find some embarrassment and bruised pride at the core of most people who resist learning new skills. If you take some pains to demonstrate to the student that s/he is a full-fledged member of the project instead of an unavoidable second stringer, you'll have their Bernie heading your way.

Don't wait until your first meeting with the student/participant to figure out how you're going to coach a skill. Take some time to plan what you'll do—e.g., set learning objectives for the session, decide how much practice you'll assign, schedule monitoring visits between coaching sessions, or figure out how frequent/long each session will be. Sure, you're a busy person with too much to do and too little time. Blocking out fifteen or twenty minutes on your to-do list for "Plan Coaching" has to hurt, but if you fumble through a coaching session, you'll pay the price in your student's resentment and in slow/no improvement.

Coaching physical skills is basically monkey see, monkey do. Demonstrate how to perform the skill from start to finish and, if it involves several steps or is particularly complicated, break it down into component segments. Once the students have seen the whole thing, demonstrate the first segment and let them do it. If they get it right, let them practice several times. If they do not perform the task correctly the first time, be patient. Demonstrate again more slowly or break the task segment down further. You will eventually coach them to do all the segments at a normal speed, but first you must bring them to mastery on each of the skill's parts.

Coaching complex thinking and action skills is a task that begins at the end. Rather than tell the rookie exactly how to do it, you begin by telling what you want to accomplish:

> *Project Manager:* As the result of negotiating our off-shore product fabrication contract, you want the other party to concede the shortest possible lead time requirement while you minimize our costs.
>
> [*or*] The result of brainstorming and problem solving our project outcome and schedule is the development of a clear course of action that will yield the highest value result in the shortest possible period of time at a cost that is equal to or less than we would pay using more conventional methods.

In the same way that you break physical skills into segments, you also break complex skills into phases with their own phase objectives:

> *Project Manager:* The first part of a successful safety benchmarking collaboration is called rapport building, where you establish enough credibility and openness with representatives from other companies that they will answer your probes.
>
> [*or*] The first phase in preparing a presentation of our

project's results is audience analysis, where you find
out who will be in attendance, what the audience
wants and needs to hear, how interested and familiar
they are with our project, and their concerns or reservations.

When the student is clear about what you're trying to accomplish, explain how you're going to proceed and demonstrate
one way (hopefully the best way) to produce a phase objective.
Afterwards, discuss what you did and why, answering any
questions and pointing out key aspects. Then let the student
practice. Afterwards, brief and practice again until the student
either demonstrates an understanding and some skill or shows
mistake-induced frustration, at which point you seize the opportunity to comfort his Bernie with words of encouragement. Build
mastery in each phase of the complex skill before you put the
phases together, and be sure to provide enough practice so that
when you send students into the lion's den of reality, they'll
have a good chance to succeed.

Coaches make three typical mistakes:

1. *Allowing the student to practice a new skill the wrong way.*
Practice doesn't make perfect; it simply makes people better at
doing whatever they practice. If they practice a mistake more
than a couple times, they will not only improve at doing it
wrong, it will be very hard for them to "forget" the wrong way
and consistently do it the right way. And because the outcomes
of complex skills are seldom obviously right or wrong, the inefficiencies or ineffectiveness that a student can learn from practicing marginally acceptable skills can be very hard to diagnose or
remedy. Take the time to coach it right and to monitor the student's practice and you'll be rewarded with peak performance.
Do anything else and you'll probably create permanent error
patterns!

2. *Declaring mastery too early.* Doing something right a couple times isn't mastery, but many impatient coaches jump the
gun before enough practice has occurred. Students, who by
definition don't know what they don't know, are not only unre-

liable judges of their own mastery, they are also eager to graduate. When their coach says they're ready to suit up and play,
even wobbly rookies are willing to agree.

3. *Talking too much.* Oral descriptions of physical behavior
are notoriously inaccurate and unhelpful. Worse, they tend to
distract the learner from the behavior s/he is trying to watch or
execute. Likewise, detailed explanations of complex skills may
help the rookie talk about the skill, but do little to help them
actually execute the skill. If you must blabber, wait until after
your student has finished practicing and try not to expect much
positive result from your descriptions. If you limit talking to
words of praise and "pay special attention to X," you'll coach
physical and complex skills much more efficiently and effectively.

Getting help from other people is more than completing a
roster of project participants. Because the success of the project
ultimately rests on your shoulders, you must do everything in
your power to be sure that each participant is ready, willing, and
able to help. If you fail to estimate their ability and motivation
beforehand and you neglect taking the actions required to shore
up any shortfalls in either or both of these essential areas, *help* is
the last thing you're likely to call what you get.

Chapter 3

Planning and Charting Projects

Every moment spent planning saves three or four in execution.

—Crawford Greenwalt, President, Dupont

It is a bad plan that admits of no modification.

—Publilius Syrus, Roman writer, c. 42 B.C.

OK," Jack thought, "now I'm ready to go. I've interviewed Fran and some end users about what they want. I've identified people who can work on the software upgrade project, and I know when I have to be finished."

With the last fact, his deadline, firmly fixed in his mind and on his planner, Jack kicked himself into overdrive. While other participants in his project worked on essential tasks like finding the telecommunication hardware required to network all the computers, modifying system code to allow different computers to link together, and preparing training modules to teach end users how this library would work, Jack took on the core task of building input screens and configuring databases. As days and weeks of work passed, Jack and his team were making what he thought was reasonable progress. Then Jack ran directly into a brick wall: help screens. One of the stakeholders had made a point of insisting that the upgrade include on-line help screens that would show users everywhere how to input data or run reports. At the time, it seemed like a reasonable request and something Jack could easily figure out as he worked on his part of the project. But when he got to the point where he actually had to have a way to pull down screens with instant answers to the dozens of possible questions, Jack quickly discovered just how difficult it would be.

After investing about a week in calls to people who might be able to help him with his problem and brainstorming with the rest of his project team, Jack decided he'd better meet with Fran to update her and ask for suggestions. As if she were reading his mind, Fran beat Jack to the punch, dropping in for a progress report just as Jack was about to head to her office. While Jack described the project status, focusing heavily on the help-screen issue, Fran's face telegraphed a range of feelings. She was obviously concerned that Jack wasn't closer to completion and that he didn't have a prototype to show her boss. Fran was also puzzled. As she would explain later, Fran couldn't figure out why Jack had spent so much time on a feature of the inventory software upgrade that only one person really wanted. And, on top of looking concerned and puzzled, Fran was visibly more than a little upset.

Working hard to contain her budding frustration with Jack, Fran let an uncomfortable silence hang in the air as the update concluded. Jack, not knowing what to say, squirmed as Fran took off her glasses and rubbed her eyes. Finally, she looked up and said, "Jack, we're in some trouble. I really expected that you'd have something to show me today. My boss expects to see something before the end of the week. Forget about the help-screen feature and figure out how you can come up with a good-looking prototype by Friday. See me before the end of the day and, Jack [*Fran's pause was almost as unsettling as her unflinching eye contact*], come with good news."

A flock of excited butterflies flew frantically in the empty space that was once Jack's stomach. But with only two hours left in the day, Jack managed to ignore them enough to ponder a bailout plan.

For People Who Don't Think They Need to Plan Projects Carefully

After his fact-finding interviews were complete, Jack figured that he had enough information to immediately brief his troops and start working. He was wrong. Although a great deal of life and work doesn't require carefully constructed plans to keep the wheels on, extending a personal quick-draw habit to project leadership is always a mistake. Nonplanners like Jack often hide their penchant for action-over-focus with self-congratulatory platitudes ("I'm a 'can do' person who embodies the American work ethic and who champions mean and lean productivity by hitting the ground running!"). But hot air notwithstanding, they too often rush toward their objective only to slip and fall or to end up in the wrong place.

Creating a plan involves assembling a project's activities and outcomes, first in your thoughts and, eventually, on paper. The act and outcomes of project plan development will yield many valuable results.

Thinking through the sequences of activity and outcomes that make up a project will yield efficiency and effectiveness as you anticipate resource needs, detect potential problems, and predict the time required for each activity. By walking through the project in your head and on paper before actually doing it in real time, you enable yourself and your project team to work faster, more skillfully, with greater confidence, and with fewer delays.

Project plans allow you to show a detailed picture of actions and outcomes to prime movers, end users, and any other constituency that you interviewed during the fact-finding phase. While your boss may be the prime mover on a project, s/he will almost always want you to produce an outcome that satisfies the widest range of interested people. By showing your project plan to those who will support the project or use its results, you give them a chance to give you more definitive feedback and commitments.

Mentors and other technical experts may have given you their ideas during fact finding, but when you show them a detailed project plan, they can give you much better reactions and suggestions. They may be able to recognize elements from a similar project that you can borrow. Or, by virtue of their experience and expertise, mentors and/or experts might be able to plug in an idea or a new technology that could improve your outcome or accelerate your progress.

"So," you may be saying to yourself, "where will I get the time for this detailed planning? My boss didn't ask for a plan; s/he asked for results!" The answer to your question is that you'll get the time from hours and weeks that would otherwise be wasted dealing with unanticipated problems and missed opportunities.

Introduction to Planning and Charting

Planning is the process of transforming all the information you've uncovered during fact-finding interviews into a course of action that is specific enough so that you and your project team won't (1) guess what to do next, (2) wonder if you will make the deadline, (3) worry that a show-stopping problem will blow the project schedule, or (4) wish that the prime mover had asked someone else to lead the project. Planning is a logical, orderly process that begins at the end.

Step 1: Goal Setting

Write, edit, discuss, and get consensus on a desired, sufficient, prudent, possible, and/or cost-effective final project outcome. In some cases, your fact finding will reveal that stakeholders (typically executive and/or management employees) and end users (employees who directly produce value) already agree on the project outcome. If that's the case, capture their consensus on paper by detailing the project outcome in a memo that includes a sentence like this: "From discussions with the people who authorized this project and those who will be using the new inventory software in our retail locations, it appears that we are all in agreement about the project outcome as it is described above." If someone has a big problem with the project outcome you've defined, they'll probably call you. Otherwise, you can move on to Step 2, the development of a milestone trail.

As you discuss your proposed project goal with stakeholders and end users, you may find that differences between what your project can reasonably produce and what they want or are willing to pay for are frequent enough (i.e., every faction wants something a little different) and/or big enough (you want to produce paper planes and they want 747s) to warrant inviting some key people to a consensus-building meeting.

Consensus building doesn't mean that at the end of one or more meetings, everybody arrives at the same conclusion. Building a consensus means that after listening to the input of everyone involved, the leader synthesizes the best possible outcome and everyone else accepts it. Therefore, if you're going to build a consensus about the project outcome, the prime mover must grant you the authority to set a project goal that s/he may not completely like. And every stakeholder, end user, and participant must be willing to support, accept, and work on producing an outcome that may not be exactly what they would prefer. Consequently, before you spend time trying to build a consensus, you need to determine whether consensus building is possible or necessary. Sit down with the prime mover and describe what you've discovered while fact finding. Call particular attention to the range of desired outcomes and try to sell the idea that forging a consensus on the project outcome will maximize its value. Producing an outcome that end users won't use, that technical experts can't support, or that customers don't like is seldom a good idea.

There are several circumstances under which building a consensus is not necessary, not possible, or both. If all the end users are in agreement about the outcome they need but the prime mover wants something different, you may be able to sell the end user's vision to the prime mover ("If that's what they need, let's give them that!"). If you can't sell the end user's preferred project outcome to the prime mover ("Jack, I'd be happy to support that, but we just can't spend that much money on this project during this fiscal year") but s/he's willing to consider an outcome that is closer to the end user's vision, you'll need to organize a meeting of stakeholders and end users to negotiate a compromise project outcome. And you may find that the prime mover is unwilling to consider modifying the project goal in any way ("Who's paying for this project, Jack?"). Faced with this lose/lose situation, if you can't sell the prime mover's goal to the end users, prepare to produce a white elephant.

If nailing down the final outcome involves consensus building, take care not to become a pork barrel politician. Building consensus doesn't mean that everyone will get what they want, so don't oversell it with unrealistic promises about the project's outcome or the resources that will be available to produce the outcome. Trying to please everyone involved will only bloat your project outcome, extend your schedule, stretch your budget, and make enemies out of people who are pressured to give you extra resources.

Building consensus isn't an electoral process littered with winners and losers; don't fall into the democratic trap of letting everyone vote for their faction's favorite outcome. If you do, you are sure to create two or more groups and only one of them will be called winners. From the moment a person becomes a loser, expect little or no support for your project.

Start consensus-building meetings with a clear statement of the various project outcome alternatives as you understand them. Because you are eventually going to forge the outcome everyone will be expected to accept, you'll need to be convincingly impartial. Once you've laid the groundwork for a balanced discussion of outcomes, encourage everyone to describe the project outcome they want and why they want it. Every involved person gets the opportunity to emphasize the merits of his or her recommendation; no one is allowed to trash the ideas or outcome recommendations of others. Your job as leader is twofold: (1) to keep the discussion focused on project outcome alternatives and how to arrive at the best possible one, and (2) to listen carefully and respond to what everyone says, which means asking questions like, "George, do you mean that the final marketing plan we develop must include a way to advertise on the Internet?" or "Then, if I understand you, Alice, the restacking of personnel here at the home office must be done in one month or less and must yield space for at least 300 more administrative staff; is that correct?"

When everyone has described their outcome preference and discussed the various outcome alternatives—which may take more than one meeting—they will have been transformed. Before consensus building, you were the only person who knew what everyone wanted. Now everyone with a stake in the project's outcome has a sense of what everyone else wants. They've also been heard, which takes much of the arbitrariness out of an outcome you could have created before consensus building. As a result of their transformation, when you thank them and let them know that you'll try to assemble the best possible outcome from their recommendations, they'll be much more likely to embrace the project goal you synthesize.

One last and very important element of consensus building is presenting the consensus goal you've synthesized, explaining it to stakeholders and end users, and asking for their commitments of support, participation, and/or use. The respect you demonstrated when you went to end users and other stakeholders for their outcome input will grow and become a two-way process when you ask for their commitment to the consensus goal.

Step 2: Developing a Trail of Milestones

With a project goal in hand, the second planning step is to develop a sequence of intermediate goals, known as milestones. Like the project goals already discussed, milestones specify the actual result of work and when it must be complete. By developing one or more sequences of milestones, you can gain commitments from your various participants that they will produce specific milestone outcomes and you can coordinate the efforts of several people who are working on a project schedule that is defined by the milestone completion dates.

Defining trails of milestones (there may be several, parallel milestone sequences going on simultaneously) involves two planning perspectives; big-to-small and back-to-front. Beginning with big-to-small, look at the project goal and ask yourself questions such as the following:

- What are the major elements of this project, and what will be the outcomes of each?

- What are the different departments or competency areas that must be involved in the project, and what part of the final outcome will they produce or support?
- What are the major phases this project must go through, and what outcome will signal the end of one phase and the beginning of the next?

Jack, after running into several of the problems that result from skimpy planning, developed the following project goal:

Develop a software upgrade for our company's existing inventory control software system that (1) reduces inputting and processing time by 50 percent, (2) can be used with no errors by new employees after no more than one hour of instruction, and (3) reduces the average number of back-ordered products by 75 percent or more. This software upgrade should be field-tested and on-line no later than April 1, 199X.

With this final goal in hand, Jack asked himself some big-to-small questions that resulted in his breaking the project into three major phases:

1. *Project preparation.* Complete when all participants have been identified, when software and hardware have been reviewed, and when new-hire training procedures for use of inventory control systems have been evaluated.
2. *Software development.* Complete when the inventory control inputting, processing, and output formatting programs have been rewritten, field-tested for accuracy, user-friendliness, inputting efficiency, and back-order reduction and have been signed off as meeting necessary standards.
3. *User handoff.* Complete when new hires and existing employees are able to use the new system to input inventory control data with no errors after one hour of training and when the new system has been loaded and successfully brought on-line in all retail locations.

With each major project phase identified, Jack looked at each through the lens of big-to-small again, labeling each outcome within the three phases:

Project Preparation

1. Complete a review of all hardware and software configurations presently being used in all our retail locations.
2. Prepare an analysis of new-hire training on inventory input procedures.
3. Identify and list all uses presently made of inventory control information.
4. Etc.

Software Development

1. Identify any bottlenecks, mistakes, or inconsistencies in existing inventory control processing code that reduce efficiency or accuracy.
2. Identify computer system upgrade plans, analyze their impact on upgraded inventory software, and describe procedures to ensure compatibility.
3. Acquire equipment to test upgraded software prototypes.
4. Etc.

User Handoff

1. Develop a one-hour training module for new hires that prepares them to use the upgraded software flawlessly.
2. Identify a list of personnel in each retail location who are qualified to install and test new software.
3. Develop measures of accuracy, efficiency, and backlog control that can be implemented at each retail location.
4. Etc.

As Jack repeatedly applies big-to-small questions to the project as a whole, to its phases, to the component elements of each phase, and so forth, he'll reach a point of diminishing returns. Jack (and you) will recognize this point when the breakdown process begins to feel like busywork. That's when you switch from a big-to-small perspective to one of back-to-front. Beginning with one of the major phase goals, sequence each outcome in that phase from project end to project beginning. Some outcomes will break apart into several components, others may combine into one, and new outcomes will in all likelihood be revealed to you. Repeat the back-to-front journey with each phase until you are satisfied that all the essential outcomes have been sequenced and that each trail of outcomes will clearly communicate performance expectations to project participants.

Step 2 is finished when you transform the outcome sequences into milestones by adding tentative completion dates to each. The word "tentative" is used because, regardless of your needs, everyone on your project will have other work for which they are committed and, in all likelihood, they will have something to say about when they can actually produce their outcome. Therefore, target milestone deadlines that are realistic but that allow you some room to make concessions to overscheduled participants. The most important aspect of setting milestone dates is to know which milestones must be met on what specific days if the project is to stay on schedule. Once you're sure of those critical milestones, you're ready to begin Step 3.

Step 3: Gaining Specific Commitments
From Participants

When harvesting milestone commitments on projects with little or no time for delays or that require the involvement of scarce resources (experts, equipment, etc.), talk to the participants who will be responsible for the most essential milestones first. Begin the meeting by describing your plan to the participants and asking them to volunteer fine-tuning suggestions to improve its efficiency, effectiveness, and/or chances for success. Although prior discussions you've had with prospective participants have provided many of the ideas and direction for your plan, this will be the first time they see the actual project blueprint, so don't miss an opportunity to fill in gaps or leverage their better-informed suggestions.

As you listen to their comments, look for that point in the discussion where you'll turn the conversation from feedback to commitments:

> ***Project Manager:*** Mary, the reason I wanted to show you the project plan is to get any final ideas you have and to finalize your group's involvement in the project. As you can see, the plan calls for the completion of a training module for new hires by February 15. Will your group be able to develop, pilot, and finalize the module as we've defined it here in the plan by then?

Because of the influencing you've been doing during fact-finding interviews, your participants will probably agree to the outcome, but you may experience some resistance on deadlines. You've got some time to concede on your milestones, but if the participant insists on a milestone deadline that would delay your project goal beyond its deadline, your options are limited to (1) brainstorming a more efficient way to produce the milestone (see Step 4, below), (2) trying to sell the milestone deadline, or (3) going to the prime mover either to access some higher-voltage authority or to get approval to push back the project deadline.

Step 4: Brainstorming the Most Efficient, Most Effective Project Activities

Some milestone-producing activities will not improve with the creative input of brainstormers—and some will. Many projects that operate on very tight schedules can be brought in on time only if creative shortcuts are taken. And, with the pace of change and technology increasing daily, projects that produce superior results often demand brand-new solutions. For those reasons, it is important to distinguish between project milestones that should be produced with tried-and-true activities and milestones that could be produced faster and/or better with a new approach.

If you decide to brainstorm, invite a diverse group to a

meeting that lasts at least an hour. In addition to the participants who are responsible for the outcome, invite some end users, assorted stakeholders, and some people whose only qualifications are their energy and creativity. You probably don't want to invite the prime mover, however, since many people clam up when they think a boss might hear them saying something stupid.

Open the meeting with a clear statement of the purpose:

> "We're here to consider various ways to produce a superior training module for the new inventory control system in three weeks."

Using some sort of visual for the brainstorming purpose may be wise, since people in the heat of creativity can drift off into tangents.

Because so many people are oriented toward problem solving rather than idea generation, explain that you don't expect or want to leave the meeting with a specific set of steps to take. You've called the session for the sole purpose of coming up with ideas, no matter how far-fetched they may sound. Then tell them the ground rules:

1. Nobody is allowed to criticize ideas.
2. Everybody is encouraged to borrow and bend each other's ideas.

3. Don't worry about taking notes—a scribe will write the ideas on a flipchart.
4. Getting up and pacing is OK.
5. If you think it, say it; volume, not apparent quality, is the desired result.

As leader, your first job is to choose a scribe who can write quickly and legibly on a flipchart. Once that person is in place, your job is to keep:

1. People from censoring ("Whoa, George, remember that *every* idea is a good one!")
2. Things going through obvious enthusiasm, which includes praising and/or giving attention to ideas ("Hey, that's great—I never thought of that!")
3. People at ease but focused during dry spells ("Nobody's talking, but I can hear the wheels turning in there!")

Brainstorming usually starts off slowly, gradually accelerates to a faster tempo, and then slows to a stop. Don't end with the first dry spell. The pressure that silence puts on people and the ideas that have been floating around the room typically combine to form a second and third burst of energy that will give you your best results. When you are convinced that you've gotten their best inspirations—usually after an hour or so—thank your brainstormers and end the meeting.

Sometimes, you and your milestone-producing participants will be able to pull out enough usable ideas from the stack of flipchart paper to create an improved milestone-producing activity. Other times, you'll have to repeat the process before a new and improved activity materializes. And, in some cases, you'll end the process convinced that the tried-and-true solution you started with is still the best one. In any case, you'll know the best way to produce the milestone in question.

Step 5: Building and Reviewing an Inventory of Necessary Resources and Approvals

Prior to developing a detailed plan, the prime mover's willingness to support your project has probably been based more on that person's assumptions about what you can pull off than on solid information about what s/he'll get and what it will cost. Now you are ready to present a clear picture of the project and ask for a fully informed commitment. Although some prime movers may not expect this preproject sign-off step, it keeps them from potentially unpleasant surprises (i.e., cost overruns, resource competitions, your unavailability as you manage the project). And keeping prime movers from experiencing unpleasant surprises is a wise thing to do.

To prepare a resource and approval budget, go through your milestones and list answers to each of these questions;

1. What resource will I need?
2. When will I need it?
3. How much of it will I need?
4. How much will it cost?
5. Who has to say yes in order for me to get it?

Take your list of needed resources to a meeting with the prime mover and review them item by item. Be prepared to defend and/or sell your needs and be clear about the necessary minimum on each resource. If the prime mover won't commit enough juice to ensure your project's success, take one of the three options available:

1. Revise the outcome downward.
2. Revise the schedule outward.
3. Revise your project leader role goneward.

Step 6: Charting the Project

Lists of milestones, goals, and activities are effective in communicating important details but are miserable when it comes to communicating a project's complexity, interdependence, and scope. To give people a glimpse of the project's big picture, you need to show them an illustration of the project, or in this case, a project chart of some kind. By developing a project chart, you will create an important communication tool to use with participants, prime movers, and others. Developing the chart will also reveal details you may have missed up to this point and can highlight potential bottlenecks and time-critical milestone/activity sequences.

Begin charting by compiling a list of the information that, for the most part, you've already gathered: work activities and the milestones that the work will produce; the time required for the activity to yield the milestone, and a new category of information called *dependencies*. A dependency exists when work to complete one milestone cannot begin until an earlier milestone has been completed.

The example shown in Figure 3-1 was built by alternately working the far right and left columns; when an obvious milestone was listed, the needed work activity was identified by answering the question, "What work is necessary in order to produce this milestone?" And when a project task was identified, the corresponding milestone space was filled by answering the question, "What will the outcome of this work be?" As the project leader kept asking and answering these questions, a number of discrete tasks and their milestones emerged.

Once the project leader was satisfied that her project to-do list didn't have any big blind spots, she made estimates of task durations based on such items as current workloads, the urgency of the whole project, and the availability of resources. Of course, she had to make tweaks in flexible tasks so that the project outcome could be scheduled to appear on the deadline, but with a little shoehorning, she completed the dependency column and the charting checklist by asking herself, "What has to happen, what milestone must be met before work can start on this particular task?"

Choosing the Right Type of Project Plan Chart

There are two general categories of project charts: (1) the Gantt chart, for the big-picture, don't-sweat-the-details approach, and (2) the project flowchart, for the nothing-falls-through-the-cracks, up-close-and-personal approach. Gantt charting is the safe and efficient choice for projects with few dependencies and routine work activities. Develop a flowchart

Figure 3-1. Project charting checklist.

Project _____ Inventory Software Upgrade _____

Deadline _____ 6-30-9X _____

Work Activities	Task Time	Activity Start Depends On	Milestone(s)
1. Fact finding	1 month	Task auth.	Planning information
2. Planning	2.5 weeks	Completion 1	Completion of Gantt
3. Approval	9 days	Completion 2	Plan approval
4. Screen development	5 weeks	Completion 3	Screen prototype ready
5. End-user test	3 weeks	Completion 4	Focus group feedback
6. Database development	7 weeks	Completion 3	Database prototype ready
7. End-user test	2 weeks	Completion 6	Focus group feedback
8. Debugging	3 weeks	Completion 5 & 7	Screen/database finals
9. Installation	5.5 weeks	Completion 8	Application installed-regions
10. User training	2.5 months	Completion 8	Corporate users trained

if your project involves (1) tight timelines, (2) unfamiliar work activities, (3) other work competing for your participants' time, (4) participants and/or supervisors whom you don't know and, most important, (5) many dependencies.

Gantt Charts

This schedule-tracking format was invented during World War I by an industrial engineer named Henry Gantt. Hank developed this monitoring tool to improve the efficiency of weapons production for the U.S. Army. He believed that by using a picture to quickly communicate a great deal of weapons production information (e.g., each project phase, its estimated duration, phase progress, and milestone accomplishment) to the workers, their productivity would improve. He was right, and today you can see Gantt's fingerprints all over the Statistical Process Control charts popularized by Total Quality Management.

Our friend Jack's Gantt chart, illustrating the phases involved in his inventory software upgrade project, appears as Figure 3-2. Jack started by listing the project activity phases from his charting checklist down the left side of a blank page and charting a timeline from the project start date through to the deadline across the bottom. After adding some vertical lines to mark off months, he drew in black rectangles that extended from the start to the estimated finish date for each phase. During the course of the project, Jack translated his estimate of the amount of progress in each phase into regularly updated black lines underneath each white rectangle.

After Jack created his first draft of the project chart, he could see that his proposed schedule would have the project end two weeks after his deadline. Instead of trying to get more time for the project, Jack went back to his chart checklist and shaved days off phases wherever he could. After tightening up his schedule, Jack made a new chart, noting milestone outcomes for particular phases in a milestone legend at the bottom of the page. He took this version to stakeholders, end users, and a couple of experienced coworkers. With their feedback, Jack adjusted the schedule and sought Fran's approval. Let's go through those steps again.

Figure 3-2. Jack's Gantt chart.

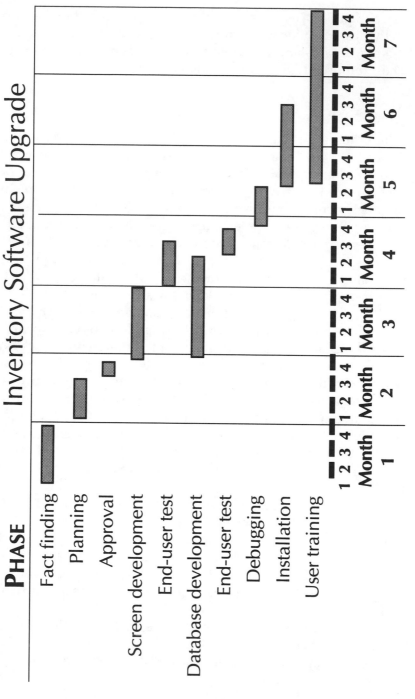

Building a Gantt Chart

1. List the phases of the project, from first to last, down the left side of a page.
2. Add a time scale across the bottom from project beginning to deadline.
3. Draw a blank rectangle for phase 1 from the phase start date to its estimated completion date.
4. Draw rectangles for each remaining phase, making sure that dependent phases start on or after the date any earlier, dependent phase finishes.
5. For phases that aren't dependent and that don't have dependencies, draw time-estimate rectangles according to the preferences of the people doing and supervising the work.
6. Adjust phase time estimates, as needed, so that the whole project finishes on or before the deadline.
7. Add a milestone legend, as appropriate.
8. Show this chart to stakeholders, end users, technical experts, collaborators, and others, as appropriate, for feedback.
9. Adjust the chart as needed.

Gantt Chart Limitations

A Gantt chart will serve you well for illustrating the major phases of a routine project and for tracking progress, but if things start unraveling, the lack of detail typical of a Gantt chart can force you to miss deadlines and/or go over budget. Here are just some of the icebergs that could turn a Gantted project into the *Titanic*.

1. *Gantt charts don't highlight when and where schedule-busting problems are likely to occur*. During the development of your charting checklist, you may have "seen" where a delayed approval, slow user feedback, or a busy collaborator's overdue input might put you behind schedule, but Gantt charts aren't designed to highlight that kind of information.

2. *If you do have a delay, a Gantt chart gives you only general information about its impact on the entire schedule and practically no information about what you can do to catch up*. If the delay is in a phase that later phases depend on, a Gantt can tell you only that the entire project will finish late by the duration of the delay; it doesn't point to a specific activity or event that if hurried up, can put you back on schedule.

3. *Gantt charts don't force you to manage your time carefully*. If you've got a two-week period to finish a phase and you are even a little prone to procrastination, you can easily find yourself letting things slide the first week and burning midnight oil for the second. More powerful charting techniques break activities and events down into shorter, discrete tasks that make managing your time and combating serious procrastination a little easier.

4. *Tracking project progress can be difficult and/or misleading*. The black rectangle that you draw under the time estimate rectangle reflects progress, not time. Half of the work in a given phase may be necessary but simple, while the remaining work could be essential and difficult. Do you fill in half of the progress bar (under your time estimate) when you've finished the easy part? If people (like your boss or an eager stakeholder) are monitoring your progress, you might be inclined to overstate your degree of completion. Or you may run into a particularly difficult phase element so that you don't fill in any more of the progress tracking line. From your stalled tracking line, do others assume that you've stopped work?

Before you decide to steer clear of conventional Gantt charts, consider a hybrid. Gantt charts can be very good for show-and-tell sessions with stakeholders and end users, so start with a nice colorful one. Then, as you identify phases where bottlenecks or missed milestone handoffs might lurk, create a flowchart (see below) that details all the individual activities and milestones that are required to keep that phase on schedule. Show the Gantt chart to people who want a nice overview, and use the flowchart to manage the phase closely and to communicate detailed information to the people supervising and/or doing the work. By developing one Gantt chart and a few well-chosen flowcharts, you'll spend more time thinking about what needs to happen and, consequently, you'll be in a much better position to manage the project and any problems that arise.

Project Flowcharts

Gantt charts are to flowcharts what magnifying glasses are to electron microscopes. Where Gantt charts illustrate the duration of phases and tell you a little about dependencies, flowcharts zoom in to show you when every project task within each phase should begin, exactly how much time is scheduled for each discrete task, when a task outcome should be complete, every task that is in progress at any given time, and all of the dependencies between outcomes, tasks, and events. Although flowcharts are more complicated to prepare, and require more in-progress tweaking, you'd be foolish not to use one if project priorities are high, timelines are short, dependencies are frequent, and delays are life threatening.

Let's start with a review of some fundamental flowchart concepts, terms, and conventions. Milestones (an intermediate outcome of the project) and events (approvals, needed tools, etc.) can trigger the start of a new project task, but they don't take time. They either appear on a particular day or they don't. It's the work that people do to create milestones that takes time. And, because it's work that takes time, it's work or activity that is represented by lines running across the flowchart time grid; the longer the time needed for work to create a particular milestone, the longer the line is.

To flowchart a simple project with a sequence of single dependencies, you would create one strand of work arrows and milestone boxes running from the starting event of the project (e.g., your boss's approval to begin) to the final project goal. To flowchart a project involving two or more work activities that were dependent on the completion of a single milestone, you would draw one work arrow ending in a milestone box that served as the starting point for two or more work arrows that ended in two or more milestone boxes. As you get into more-complex projects, flowcharting will require orchestrating several simultaneous phases, each with a few work-milestone sequences that may well interact periodically. When the tasks and outcomes of a project get to this level of complexity, a flowchart is the only way you'll be able to see, manage, and adjust what should be happening today, tomorrow, and next week.

Simple tasks are like one-person footraces: The gun fires and you start running until you cross the finish line. Projects where several people are responsible for several interdependent tasks are like long and complicated relay races. In some parts of a project relay race, runner 2 can't start until runner 1 roars up the track and hands off the baton (outcome). In other parts of the race, runner 12 can't start until runners 11, 11(a), and 11(b) all arrive and give her their batons. And in still other parts of the race, runners 14, 14(a), and 14(b) can't start until runner 13 hands off a part of his baton to each of the three waiting runners. By creating a project chart, you'll think through each of these handoffs and illustrate them so that:

1. You can proactively manage hazardous handoffs.
2. Project participants can see the horrible, schedule-busting consequences of missing their individual deadlines.
3. Supervisors and other priority predators can be shown why they shouldn't deprioritize a direct report's project involvement at a critical juncture.

Building a Project Flowchart

You don't have to build project flowcharts with rulers and pens. Several software packages exist for the sole purpose of building project flowcharts from information you input. All you have to do is input the task, milestone, dependency, and time estimate information you've gathered, and like magic they can synthesize a stunning, full-color, networkable chart. Even better, when one of your participants is abruptly right-sized into a new vocational horizon, you can tweak the project schedule file, press the "Chart Me" button, and, shazzam, you have a new and perfectly accurate flowchart.

This segment is intended for the reader who (1) doesn't have or know where to get project charting software, (2) doesn't have and/or like computers, or (3) thinks that the only way to internalize the fine art of project charting is to build one him- or herself from scratch.

As with Gantt charts, developing a project chart checklist is the first step of flowcharting. With her checklist in hand, the project leader turned a blank sheet of paper sideways, and began transforming the checklist into a flowchart (see Figure 3-3), one box at a time. She started by planting the project goal in a box located in the middle of the right side. Next, she drew a time scale across the bottom of the page, noting the project deadline date under the goal box, the project kickoff date at the far left of the timeline, and dates indicating the time available for the project evenly spaced across the page. Looking to the checklist, she saw that the project milestones and work broke out into four distinct elements involving marketing, production, administration, and information services. Working with one functional element at a time, she entered each milestone in a row, starting with the milestone that was closest to the project goal and working backwards toward the present.

Once all of the milestones were in place, the project leader returned to the first milestone she had entered and looked to the dependency column of the checklist to determine where the arrow to that milestone was coming from. After she added the arrows (with work labels and time estimates), she reviewed her chart to see if the amount of time between one milestone and the next was equal to or greater than the estimated time required by the task that was to produce the milestone. Finding one task that was estimated to take longer to produce a milestone than the schedule would permit, she called the participant responsible

Figure 3-3. Project chart flowchart.

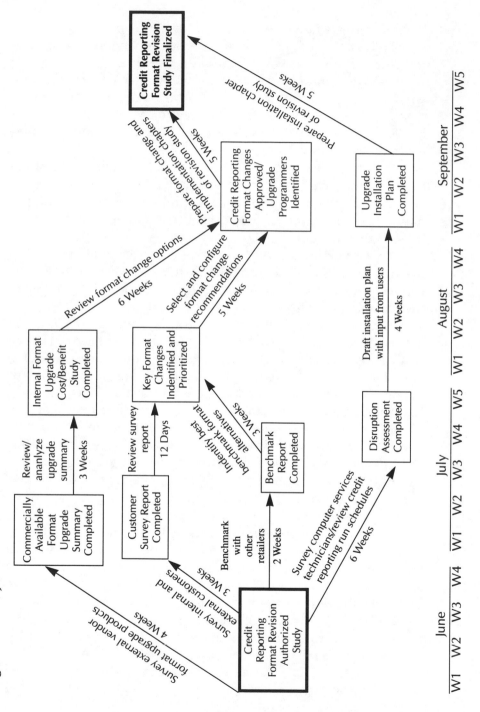

for the milestone and negotiated the involvement of some additional participants. She then shortened the task duration estimate to reflect the change.

When she was finished, she looked at her chart and said "Wow, what a mess!" So, still struggling with an overworked need to be neat, she used her first flowchart sketch as a guide for her second, positioning boxes and lines to make the best use of the available space on the page. When she finished, she had a project road map that showed her all the main thoroughfares toward success and many of the places she could expect serious traffic jams.

Let's consider some quirks, truths, and limitations of flowcharting you should keep in mind. Don't worry about neatness on the first charting attempt; it isn't going to happen and it isn't that important. All you want to do is capture the milestone boxes and work arrows accurately enough so you can produce a better illustration the second time. If you struggle to make everything look nice during your first charting run-through, you'll end up thinking more about appearances than improvements. This goes double for anyone who attempts to create a project chart with a computer drawing program. Trust me, don't worry about how it looks until you're satisfied that it accurately communicates the scope and flow of the project.

Ideally, flowcharts show the flow of work and outcomes over time. A key convention of this ideal is that outcomes don't take time and work does. Unfortunately, when you draw a big ol' outcome box on your charting grid, it can easily span several days on the timeline. Which means that you could have an arrow representing work that is shorter than the outcome box it runs into. What can you do? Short of getting really good at writing really little, there are three typical approaches. First, you can replace each outcome box description with a single letter and add a letter/outcome legend at the bottom of the page. While this option reduces the easy access impact of a project chart, it helps you accurately illustrate any intricate dependencies that might exist. Second, you could adjust the time scale of the chart so that legible, boxed outcome notations would only take up one day. This option makes for a much more accessible chart, but also makes for one that could become very long. (Some say that the flowchart for the construction of the Grand Coulee Dam was 10 feet high and 300 feet long!) Third, you could remove the chart timeline altogether and list task durations along each arrow. Of course, this does compromise the very important time-illustrating dimension of a chart, but it allows you to illustrate dependencies and indicate milestones clearly, on something more manageable than a roll of wrapping paper.

If your question has simply changed from "What can I do?" to "Which chart compromise should I choose?" let's get prescriptive. If you've got a complicated, frequently interdependent project that lasts for months, go for the letter-substitution option. It's easier to see the exact days when handoffs must occur and should be monitored. And, with managers who might pull a participant at the wrong time, the high-detail letter substitution type of chart shows them how that action would crater the work of dozens of others.

If you're working with participants and/or stakeholders who are neither patient nor project-savvy, a fully detailed (really long) chart will keep them informed with a minimum of supplementary explaining. Hang it on a wall and encourage participants to visit it. Send segments of it to key people as updates during the course of the project. But to save yourself time and trouble, don't create it by hand. The updates and adjustments will eat your schedule like a hungry dog! Put it in a computer and let it spit out revisions the quick way.

If you've got a team of reasonably disciplined time managers working on your project, use the duration notation on the arrow approach. While a proactive, priority-oriented participant is central to most successful projects, if your team puts their project duties in a personal work schedule and works that scheduled plan reliably, their disciplined approach toward work will allow you to use a project chart with less visual impact. In short, select the chart style that gives participants and stakeholders the information they need to ensure that they do what they need to do when they need to do it. That may mean using more than one flowchart, or using a Gantt chart to overview and a flowchart to manage, or it might call for something really creative. For example, a collaborator-highlighting flowchart is a combination of Gantt and flowchart styles that centers a viewer's attention on who must do what by when. If you are working with one or more collaborators who are physically separated and/or aren't used to working with others on projects, a collaborator-highlighting chart will draw their attention to who is responsible for producing or coproducing which milestones and when discrete tasks depend on the milestones that are produced by others. See Figure 3-4.

With the collaborator-highlighting flowchart, you can forcefully illustrate the impact of missed deadlines on everybody involved without having to go into lengthy (and potentially unpleasant) discussions. You would simply meet with your prime mover and data support person before beginning the task, find out if the task schedule, as illustrated, is acceptable to them, promise that you will make all your deadlines, and get them to confirm that they will make all of theirs.

Figure 3-4. A collaborator-highlighting project flowchart.

	June				July					
1234567891011121314151617181920212223242526272829301234567891011121314151617181920212223242526272829303 1
You	A		C		E	G		J K	M	N
Prime Mover		B		D	F			L		
Data Support						H	I			

Milestone Legend*

	You	Prime Mover	Data Support
A	Receive authorization		
B		Provide criteria listing	
C	Complete draft proposal		
D		Provide written draft comments	
E	Finalize proposal		
F		Approve proposal	
G	Configure data fields and		
H	begin report dvmt		Begin data analysis runs
I			Complete data runs
J	Receive data analysis		
K	Present preliminary report		
L		Provide written comments	
M	Begin final report		
N	Present and deliver final report		

*The purpose of the flowchart legend is to help project team users of every stripe understand who is doing what, with whom, and when.

Problem Solving With Project Charts

You're much more prepared to succeed now that you've gone through project planning in your head and on paper. But that doesn't mean that you're ready to start. When you've finished your project plan, you're ready to use it to identify and solve potential problems before they can gum up your schedule or chew up your outcomes.

The first place on your flowchart to look for potential problems is along the *critical path,* the single sequence of work activities and milestones that takes the longest estimated time from start to finish. Like a doctor who hovers over a patient in critical condition, much of your project management attention should be devoted to hovering over each task and outcome along the critical path. If any task or outcome takes a turn for the worse, your project is on its way to intensive care. Because any delays in producing milestones that lie in the critical path will automatically delay the accomplishment of your project goal, you must be ready to implement emergency procedures at the first sign of trouble. By putting extra energy into anticipating delays and by planning catch-up alternatives for critical path tasks and milestones, you will be better prepared to save your project's life.

Next, examine dependent milestones and the task or tasks that produce them. Pay special attention to milestones that depend on the results of two or more discrete tasks because they have a greater risk of fumbled handoffs. Isolate tasks that are unusual enough to make time estimates questionable. For example, if someone brainstormed a new way to produce a project milestone, assume that the new task will take longer than estimated.

Take some time to think about your project plan in terms of the participants who will be producing time-sensitive milestones. Are they methodical, organized, dedicated, and reliable superstars who are sure to deliver, or are they like most human beings? Rookies sometimes have trouble learning new things fast enough to turn out results on time, and seasoned veterans are sometimes so much in demand that they have trouble making multiple deadlines. Procrastinators are addicted to the excitement of deadlines, while perfectionists resist ending a task until it is absolutely perfect. If you find a fallible human collaborating on a dependent milestone that lies on the critical path, start problem solving.

Step 7: Holding a Project Plan Review Meeting

The greater the predictable problems will be if the project runs over schedule or budget, the more important it is to hold a project plan review meeting with project collaborators, stakeholders, end users, technical experts, and creative coworkers. The meeting is important because your project:

1. Doesn't need schedule-busting, surprise problems
2. Will run more smoothly if participants feel a sense of ownership over the plan and the schedule they're working on
3. Depends on everyone honoring specific commitments of support and involvement

The meeting is potentially dangerous because heavy-duty tinkerers can deconstruct your plan, bushwackers can generate questions and resistance about your project, and one person who is unwilling to commit to a schedule can lead the way for other mutineers.

The life-or-death potential for this meeting brings the following decision rule into clear relief. If you believe that key project players are anything but ready and eager, meet with them one-on-one for a discussion of the plan, and for minor adjustments of their tasks, outcomes, and/or commitments. This obviously takes longer than a single meeting but protects the considerable time you've already invested in the project.

If you are confident that a meeting would be relatively hazard-free, invite participants, stakeholders, and people who might have something to contribute to the prelaunch review. Send a memo (Figure 3-5) that includes the meeting agenda and expresses your understanding that their time is important and that you will not waste it. The following steps should help you set up and pull off an effective prelaunch review.

Figure 3-5. Meeting-invitation memo.

Date: xx/xx/xx

To: Friends of [*name of project*]

From: [*your name*]

Re: Review of Plans for [*name of project*]

I need your help. I am putting the finishing touches on the plans for [*name of project*], and, because of its importance to you and to [*names of end users*], I want to make sure the project is as efficient and productive as possible. Because of your [expertise/interest/range of knowledge], please help me by reading the information attached and by attending the meeting. I know your schedule is full, but if you could invest ninety minutes to help me put the finishing touches on the project plan, I'm sure everyone involved would benefit from your insights.

Meeting Objectives
    1. To fine-tune and finalize the plan and schedule for [*name of project*]
    2. To confirm project participation and support

Agenda

    Overview of project: 10 minutes

    Identify, discuss, and resolve any project problems; recommend, discuss, and plug in project plan enhancement: 60 minutes

    Review project schedule and confirm individual participation and support: 20 minutes

[*Add time, place, and RSVP information to the memo and send it out to the people on your list.*]

Begin the meeting on time and with a carefully rehearsed, ten-minute overview that includes background information from your fact finding and a visual representation and/or handout of your project chart. Leave time to answer questions.

Begin the second agenda item like this by asking participants:

> ***Project Manager:*** Please take the next five minutes to look for and note any ideas or suggestions that could improve this plan. That might include identifying potential problems we could plan our way around, refining a stage of the project to be more efficient, using resources more effectively, using better approaches or resources that haven't been included so far, or deleting steps or replacing aspects of the plan that you think are bound to lead to delays or other problems. Don't spend a lot of time writing out your thoughts; notes will be fine.

After five minutes have elapsed, go around the group and ask each person to explain one item (e.g., problem, enhanced procedure, better resource, faulty approach) at a time. List the items on a flipchart until all the ideas have been exhausted. Then spend as much time as you consider necessary and productive getting clarification about the listed problems and opportunities.

Next, adjust the project plan to capitalize on the suggested enhancements and avoid the serious problems raised during the discussion. Your objective for this meeting is to leave with a finalized project plan, so if at all possible, tweak the plan rather than make major changes.

Save the last five to ten minutes to review the tweaked project plan, highlighting adjustments and confirming that the plan meets with their approval and has their support. Then ask everyone to pull out their daily schedulers to confirm their availability on the days they need to work on the project. Be sure to end the meeting on time, thanking everyone for their help.

Make follow-up phone calls to everyone, thanking them individually and asking them about any problems/opportunities they may have identified but didn't have time to discuss. You may well get some good stuff during these conversations, so take notes as you talk.

Write a meeting summary and distribute it to the participants, noting the problems/opportunities that were identified and the solutions that were offered. If needed, include a revised project chart with the summary. Thank the participants for their help and send a copy to your boss and to the participants' bosses.

Is this degree of review, summary, commitment confirmation, and follow-up necessary for every project you do? Of course not. But if the consequences and likelihood of a mid-project meltdown are great enough, the two or three hours of total time spent on working on these details are cheap insurance.

Step 8: Maintaining Regular Project Reviews

Begin the process of regular project reviews by sending the prime mover a memo that signals that the project has begun. Regular project reviews are important, and beginning this form of documentation with a kickoff memo ensures that you will document the project from beginning to end.

Step 9: Relying on Your Daily Scheduler

Integrate the plan activities, schedule, review meetings, monitoring requirements, and any other project management task into your daily scheduler. You'll work your project charts during the project, but your final source for project and normal work activity should be your daily scheduler.

Chapter 4

Reviewing the Project Plan With the Prime Mover

Take nothing for granted.

—Ralph Waldo Emerson

Which of you, intending to build a tower, sitteth not down first and counteth the cost, whether he have sufficient to finish it?

—New Testament, Luke 14:28

The knot in the pit of Jack's stomach had appeared the first day he realized that the project was behind schedule, and it had been growing ever since. Its growth was especially noticeable during the decidedly downbeat meeting Jack had just left, when he had to tell Fran that he wasn't going to have the demo program to show her boss anytime soon.

If he had been listening to anything other than his own musings when he'd left Fran's office, Jack would have heard the sound of pigeonlike button pecking. Fran lost no time getting the news to her boss that the inventory upgrade deadline had to be pushed back a month because of "system compatibility problems." In one sense, this excuse was entirely true; Fran was feeling much less compatible with Jack than she had only a week before. Jack had waded into C-level details of the project so far and for so long that milestone dates slipped and the original project deadline was doubtful. If Jack had discussed the project's plan with Fran before he got under way or had reviewed project progress with Fran during the first month, she could have counseled him to make the new software system work first and to make it look pretty after the deadline date was assured. But the process of carefully planning the project had convinced Jack that his path to the deadline was not only a good one but the only one. Wrong again.

Once Jack had invested a few weeks of his life in the project, he, like most achievement-oriented people, developed a sense of ownership over it that was only strengthened by the planning process; Jack came to see himself in the driver's seat speeding toward a big success. Actually, however, Jack was only the chauffeur; Fran owned the car and expected to be told where it was going and how it was getting there. In his eagerness to accomplish important results and to recover some of his lost self-esteem, Jack was about to forget some very important facts:

1. It was Fran who initiated the software upgrade project, not Jack.
2. Jack's newly minted plan was based on the ideas and desires of a number of people in addition to Fran.
3. Although he had written the plan, he had to show it to Fran, informing her of exactly what he intended to do.
4. If Fran disagreed with what he was trying to accomplish or how he was trying to accomplish it, she could stop him dead in his tracks at any time.

In the last chapter, you were encouraged to end the planning process with a prime-mover plan review meeting. In this chapter, we explain exactly why that is so important and how you can go about doing that and more.

Seven Good Reasons to Do Initial and Periodic Project Reviews

Reason 1: So Your Prime Mover Knows What You're Doing

Projects can take up a major portion of any person's workday. Although you must exercise a fair amount of good judgment in deciding what to work on at any given time, a big part of your boss's job is to know what you're doing and to give you needed guidance. If your prime mover isn't also your boss, you'll need to keep both of these decision makers appraised of your workload and your progress.

Reason 2: So Your Prime Mover Knows How Much and in What Directions His or Her Original Intentions Have Been Modified

The project's prime mover got this effort going because s/he had an outcome in mind. As you did your planning, how that outcome will be produced and, perhaps, what that outcome will look like may have evolved through the input of end users and interested others. Now is an excellent time to make sure that your plans and your prime mover's desires haven't drifted too far apart.

Reason 3: So Your Prime Mover Can Knowingly and Comfortably Commit Resources

Up to this point, your prime mover has probably applied 80 percent of his/her thoughts about this project to its outcome and maybe 20 percent of those thoughts to how you will accomplish those outcomes. That's only natural; up to this point, there wasn't a clear, step-by-step plan to take the project from intentions to results. But now, with the project blueprint in hand, you are prepared to ask for and justify more time, help, equipment, and/or a budget.

Reason 4: So Your Boss Can Set the Priority of the Project Outcome

The chances are that you have plenty to do in addition to this project. Important deadlines might be coming up and other essential work may be requiring large amounts of your time and attention already. With this project added to your workload, some tweaking of your schedule is probably in order. With a plan in hand, you should include your boss in priority resetting so you can be confident that you're working on the right things at the right times for the right durations. Of course, if your boss and the project prime mover aren't the same people, you may need to negotiate your work priorities with both of them.

Reason 5: So You Can Avoid Breaking the Number-One Rule of Employee–Prime Mover Relationships—No Surprises

Managers earn much of their salaries by knowing what's going on with their groups, anticipating productivity problems, and minimizing expensive solutions. Capable managers prefer good news but welcome bad news if it comes before the actual disaster occurs. By doing initial project reviews, you make sure that the prime mover knows what direction you're headed in and how you intend to proceed so s/he can anticipate what you'll be doing and accomplishing. In periodic reviews of project progress, you update your prime mover so s/he isn't surprised by problems, shortfalls, or any other off-plan happenings.

Reason 6: So Your Prime Mover Can Champion Your Project to Others

Some projects come to completion in a flash of glory while others slip slowly into the half-done swamp of obscurity. Many times, the key difference between glory and obscurity is whether a prime mover is fully prepared to sell others on continued project support. In this day of rapidly shifting priorities, the use of time, expertise, and resources demanded by one project can be challenged by competing project ideas. That means your prime mover needs to know and champion, in glowing detail, the benefits of the project for everyone affected.

Reason 7: So You Can Cement Your Prime Mover's Commitment to the Project

Enthusiasm for some projects, and particularly those that take weeks and months to complete, can wane as the project transitions from the honeymoon stage to the old-married-couple mode. If prime movers haven't made and/or aren't reminded of their explicit commitment to the project, they may begin thinking about a divorce when a new, exciting project prospect catches their eye. As in good marriages, a long-running project will bear fruit if it is founded on a solemn commitment and regularly nurtured with good communication.

Three Key Times to Do Project Reviews

There are three types of project reviews: initial, periodic, and emergency. For many of the reasons listed above, the first and most important time to do a project plan review is before you begin. One of the topics you'll want on the initial review agenda is scheduling periodic project reviews. Depending on the priority of the entire project and the amount of time scheduled to complete it, you may want to schedule weekly, biweekly, or monthly project status reviews. Or you may want to tie periodic review dates to particular project milestones. In any case, come to the initial project review meeting prepared with a conservative (think CYA) periodic review schedule. And don't leave the initial review meeting without confirming and coordinating a periodic review schedule in both of your daily planners.

If your project yields the milestones you've planned on schedule and without the use of extra resources (i.e., more budget than planned or additional help from others), you won't need to ask for the third type of review (emergency). If an unanticipated problem comes up and is likely to impact budget, schedule, or outcome, you'll need to be ready to conduct an emergency review. Knowing how to conduct each type of review efficiently and effectively will be very important to your project's security, so let's consider the best process for each.

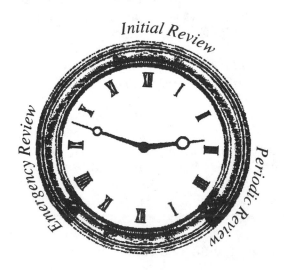

Doing Initial Project Reviews

Think meeting. Not the informal, overly spontaneous gatherings where businesspeople converse about work. Initial project reviews should be real meetings with an objective and an agenda. Although, in all likelihood, you'll be having a one-on-one meeting with a person you know, that's no excuse for winging it. Since you've invested time and energy in fact finding and in planning, show off your work to its greatest advantage by conducting a carefully planned initial review meeting. You have a number of important outcomes to nail down during this review, and if you don't prepare to accomplish them, you probably won't. Figure 4-1 shows the objectives and agenda for a typical initial review meeting. Let's take a few moments to examine its components.

Explaining the Project Plan

The first objective is the absolute minimum outcome that you can accept from an initial review meeting: that the prime mover be fully informed. If there are any misunderstandings or if you leave any important activities or events out of the explanation, unpleasant surprises will happen.

What you really want from this review, however, is described in the second objective. You want involvement, enthusiasm, support, and commitment. You want your boss to like what you're doing and how you're doing it. The planning you've done so far will help you with that objective, but your enthusiasm and some probing ("What's your impression of our plan?" or "Don't you think the plan has really shaped up into a new and better way to produce our outcome?") are also important ingredients in getting enthusiastic buy-in.

Beginning the review meeting with a summary of fact-finding information brings the prime mover up to speed on what you've discovered since s/he gave you the project assignment. You may want to divide this background into two categories: the expected and the unexpected. What did you find out that confirmed the prime mover's interest in doing the project and what did you find out that adjusted the way it should be done, the outcome(s) that are targeted, and/or the urgency with which the task should be pursued?

Figure 4-1. Initial project review agenda.

Objectives

1. To fully explain the project plan
   - Fact-finding information
   - Planned activities
   - Scheduled events and milestones
   - Resource needs
   - Potential problems
2. To solicit the prime mover's
   - Ideas
   - Feedback
   - Recommendations
   - Schedule assistance
   - Approval and commitment

Agenda Items

1. Fact-finding background information
2. Project objective
3. Project plan overview (big to little)
   - Activities and duration
     • Phases or activity sequences
     • Duration and percentage of your total time
   - Events and handoffs
     • Milestones
     • Dependencies
4. Potential problems
5. Resource needs
6. Approval and commitment

Clarifying the Project Goal

With this background information clearly described, you'll be in a good position to transition to the project goal that you've planned to accomplish. Be absolutely sure that your prime mover understands the project goal completely, particularly where it differs from the goal s/he gave you originally. The only way you can be entirely sure the prime mover fully understands the project goal is by probing him or her about specifics ("Do you see how we've expanded the number of potential users for this project outcome?" "You do realize that the shortened time-line and reduced budget for the project as it is planned here will also limit the market potential of its final outcome, don't you?"). When you're talking about the outcome that the prime mover has bought and will pay for, you must be sure s/he understands what s/he's going to get; knowing smiles and head nods aren't enough!

Explaining Project Activities and Milestones

With a firm mutual understanding of the project's goal, you're ready to whip out your project chart. Some prime movers will want you to walk them through each activity and milestone while others will prefer a couple of minutes to examine it for themselves before you go into explanations. Ask the prime mover which s/he'd prefer ("This is the plan in chart form; would you like me to walk you through it or would you rather look it over before I get into the details?").

Begin your overview by pointing out the major project phases, one at a time, from beginning to end. If your plan is anything short of painfully logical, explain why you've designed the work/milestone sequences as you have. In some cases your prime mover will only need to review your plan chart to be fully informed, while in other cases you'll have to go into more detail to be sure s/he follows your intended approach. Use the big-to-small method in overviewing your project plan; give enough information to ensure a clear understanding without dwelling on the obvious so long that your prime mover nods off.

Explaining Time Requirements

Because your prime mover is frequently also your boss and because s/he is responsible for your efficiency and productivity, you'll want to give some idea of the time demanded by the proj-ect on a daily and/or weekly basis. This is particularly true if the time required to manage this project will impact your normal work or other projects ("As you know, I'm scheduled to com-plete the data field prototypes for the reformatting task on the

11th. If I launch this project as planned, I'll be lucky to finish the prototypes by the 14th. Do you see that as a problem?"). By highlighting time-required information, your prime mover/boss (1) will have a much better idea of your level of productivity, (2) can fine-tune your project or normal work plans to match his or her sense of urgency, and (3) can make better decisions about additional resources that could be applied to the project.

Forging a Periodic Review Schedule

Now it's time to agree on a periodic review schedule. With routine projects, you may want to suggest a regular weekly review done either face-to-face or via memo. But with projects that involve new work activities, extensive resources, high costs, and/or urgently needed outcomes, it will be important to tie periodic reviews to key project milestones. Reviewing the project status when tangible measures of progress are due will enhance your prime mover's peace of mind as well as increase your motivational level. With milestones as the centerpiece of a periodic review, you can't just talk about what you've been doing; you have to show the prime mover something that you've either completed or you haven't. There's a wonderfully focusing effect that tangible milestones have on review meetings.

Highlighting Potential Delays

From milestone events, you can easily transition to handoff/dependency danger zones: points in your plan (and on your chart) where the accomplishment of a milestone triggers the beginning of project activity by someone else. As we've said before, this is where most delays happen, so if your project has one or more handoffs, you need to spend some time discussing and "what-ifing" them. If the handoff involves your prime mover—e.g., s/he must produce a piece of equipment or an approval for the project to continue—ask if s/he foresees any problem with the amount of time allotted for the activity or if the particular dates upon which s/he is supposed to do something are free enough so s/he can easily get that part done. If asking your prime mover this kind of question ("As you'll notice, I've planned for you to review the draft version on the 18th and 19th and to give me feedback on the 20th; is that enough time or should I adjust that date?") makes you uncomfortable, it shouldn't. It's much better for you and your boss to get all expectations out on the table than for you to allow him or her to overlook the prime mover role in the project's success. By asking prime movers the question, you give them a great opening to adjust their schedules if need be and you seriously reduce the chances of embarrassing them when they cause a delay and/or delay the completion of the project.

Identifying Potential Problems

By the time you finish highlighting handoffs, you'll be well into discussing potential problems. Begin this item by asking your prime mover for feedback ("I've identified five aspects of the project that I think could grow into problems; I'd like to tell you how I intend to handle them and get your reactions and ideas"). Since a great deal of project work involves problem solving, think carefully before choosing the problems that you present to your prime mover. Highlight potential problems that s/he can help you with either because of his or her experience, technical expertise, or access to other resources. Your objectives in bringing out potential problems are to let your prime mover know that you've planned carefully enough to be able to anticipate problems and to get whatever help you can to either solve the problems or to minimize their impact. Most prime movers are excellent, experienced problem solvers with a secret weapon, a fresh perspective on the project plan you're revealing to them. Make use of it.

Many times, problems can be resolved by the application of additional resources. If there are any resources you'll need in addition to those that are readily available to you or that your prime mover has already committed, list and justify them now. Include equipment, clerical support, additional computer time and/or any other resource that can ensure meeting your deadline or securing the quality of your outcome. When you've finished asking, go back over the list quickly, indicating what s/he has promised you and when you'll expect to get/use it.

Getting Approval and Commitment

The last initial review agenda item is "Approval and Commitment." Any one of the probes in Figure 4-2 can be used to confirm that your prime mover (1) believes that your plan is a good one and (2) that s/he wants you to move forward with the project. Asking for a clear go-ahead may serve two purposes. First, it may smoke out an objection. Think of it in terms of the minister's wedding invocation: "If there is anyone among us who can give cause why this marriage should not be entered into, speak now or forever hold your peace." And, second, as we observed earlier, once your prime mover says yes to your plan, s/he is much more likely to champion your project steadfastly.

Figure 4-2. Steps in asking the prime mover for a project commitment.

Minor Point

"Would next Monday be soon enough to start the project?"

Open Close

"This project certainly gives us a great opportunity to leapfrog the competition, don't you think?"

Alternative Choice

"Would you like me to wait until I brief the others involved before I start, or should I get at it immediately?"

Inducement

"Because of the short timeline on this project, I'd like to get your go-ahead today if at all possible."

Sharp Angle

"Unless you have a reservation, I plan on starting this project first thing tomorrow morning."

Doing Periodic Project Reviews

Think KISS (Keep It Short and Simple). Because nothing of grave importance has altered the cost, resource requirements, or outcome of the project, this review can be conducted in a brief, one-one-one meeting or in a short memo (if something grave had happened, you wouldn't be waiting until a periodic review to communicate it). Brevity is the soul of wit and of periodic reviews, so limit this updating event to four topics:

1. *What it is.* Summarize the project and its deadline. Your prime mover may have a number of people doing a range of projects, so begin with an orienting paragraph to let him/her zero in on this particular project:

> This memo is an update of the marketing focus group project that is targeting customer preferences in leisure wear. It will provide project status information as of the 14th of March, 199X.

2. *How it's doing.* Describe the project's current status, focusing almost exclusively on the budget and schedule. If the project is going smoothly, this part can be handled in a single paragraph:

> Seven of the twelve scheduled focus groups have been conducted in our two target markets. Information from those sessions has been forwarded to the test construction team in information services, who are creating survey questions. All involved participants report being on schedule as of this week.

3. *How it has evolved.* Explain any minor changes or adjustments to the original plan. If your schedule slipped because of delays, explain who, what, and why. If you needed additional resources, what were they, how much of them were required, and what was the impact on the project budget. And if you expect plan variances to have an impact on the outcome, what is that impact and what have you done or can you do to minimize the downside? If, after composing the following paragraph, you

think the prime mover's first reflex would be to dial you up, put down your pen and beat a path to his or her door; it's emergency review time.

> Because of the unanticipated illness of two of the focus group facilitation team, an external consultant was retained for two days to lead two focus groups. This expense will be absorbed in our travel budget and should not impact the final project cost.

4. *What's going to happen next.* Looking into your crystal ball, what can you foresee happening between now and the deadline? Although you don't want to burden your prime mover with problems you expect to solve, if you can foresee problems that could require prime mover involvement, it's better to preview them now than wait for the emergency to happen.

Doing Emergency Project Reviews

The key difference between a problem and a disaster is time: the time to solve the problem that you foresee versus no time to do anything but eat the budget overrun or push the deadline back. Since most projects involve many problems that must be worked through, it can be difficult to distinguish between the ones that you can solve and those that will not yield without some unplanned help. Below are the key steps to take in an emergency project review.

1. As soon as you realize that the problem is going to keep you from meeting your deadline and/or finishing at or under budget, get an appointment with your boss. Whether s/he can help you with the problem or not, your boss (or prime mover) should be the first to know about the emergency. This interaction is best handled face-to-face, but if your boss is going to be out of the office for any period of time (i.e., more than twenty-four hours), do the emergency review via phone.

2. Unless you have reason to believe that s/he is already informed and current, quickly bring your boss up to speed on the project and its status. For example:

> ***Project Manager:*** As you know, we've been working on the inventory software upgrade project for the past three weeks, building and testing the code component for an easy entry–easy access database. Presently, I'm conducting end-user testing of the input screens.

3. Explain the problem, what you've done to solve the problem, and how much impact it will have on the project if you continue to work as planned:

> ***Project Manager:*** The problem I'm having is that the end users who promised to test the screens and provide me with feedback are entirely unavailable. I talked to Phil Jones, who had promised twenty-five of his people to spend a day each testing the screens, and he has almost completely backed out. He says that a new high priority task has been handed off to him and he can't spare a person for at least the next thirty days. After begging and pleading with him, I tried five other managers who have people who could test the screens. I got a total of four testers for one day each. If I can't get at least fifteen more tester days by the end of this week, I can't possibly make the deadline as planned.

4. As a general rule, your next step is to present options. Of course, some boss/prime movers are such experienced problem solvers that they'll be way ahead of you, but being ready with options at this point is much better than just stopping while the monkey on your shoulders hops over to your boss's back:

> ***Project Manager:*** As I see it, there are three options. I could park the project until Phil's people are available. Or, I could debug using the feedback from the four testers I've scrounged up. Or, perhaps you could talk to Phil about letting me have some of his people for testing. What do you think?

5. Your boss/prime mover may immediately elect one of your proposed options or s/he may want to generate some addi-

tional alternatives. Whichever the case, make absolutely sure that you (1) listen carefully, (2) discuss the implications of each option on the project's schedule, budget, and outcomes, and (3) confirm final decisions by restating them at the end of the review:

> *Project Manager:*   Let me go through this to make sure I've got everything. I will have the four testers I've lined up do their work with the screens tomorrow. In the meantime, you'll try to recruit as many more testers as possible for at least four hours each. I'll be prepared to run each one of them through the screen test sequence whenever they say they're available. Debugging starts next Wednesday, using whatever screen-test data I've been able to gather between now and then. And I'll pick up the two lost days during the training phase. Is that correct?

6. Inform everybody who is affected by a schedule, budget, or outcome change. The people who don't play an active role in the remainder of the task will need only a memo telling them what happened (be general enough to avoid embarrassing anyone) and what the adjustments are. People who must play some active role (a collaborator, a stakeholder, a feedback giver) should be contacted in person so that you can reconfirm their availability.

In discussions with hundreds of project managers and project participants, the lifeline function of good communication with prime movers is regularly reinforced. Whether in postmortems of failed projects or analyses of projects that succeeded, proactive "managing up" by the project leader to the prime mover was consistently cited as central to the project's outcome. The moral of the story is to keep your project plugged into the people who turned it on; that way you're much more likely to bring in a winner.

Chapter 5

So Much to Do, So Little Time

To choose time is to save time.

—Francis Bacon

Time is the scarcest resource and unless it is managed, nothing else can be managed.

—Peter Drucker

A hound dog tracking a scent. Yes, that's what Jack felt like this morning and it felt good. Years earlier, a friend at work made a joke about how much Jack resembled the friend's English foxhound. Just like a hound dog following the scent of a fox, whenever Jack zeroed in on a task, nothing distracted him and very little could slow him down until he ran down his quarry. With the inventory upgrade project chart posted on his wall and Fran's feedback still lodged in his memory, Jack was ready to bark a couple of times and start running down his activity-milestone trail. Then the phone started ringing.

Other tasks Jack was involved in needed his input; meetings about new equipment requirements had to be attended; associates with problems had to be helped; and before Jack knew it, 8 A.M. was just a memory and Jack was worried that somewhere Elvis was singing about him. With the mountain of work that was already on his plate and the last-minute requests for his time heating up his phone, how could Jack ever stay on schedule with his inventory upgrade project?

Even ruthless time managers have a hard time getting the maximum productivity out of every day, so it is little wonder that people who use the time management habits they've collected haphazardly through life almost always find themselves with too much to do, too little time, and a gnawing feeling of underperformance.

In this chapter, we're going to learn how to take the hard planning work you've done so far and fit it into your already busy workday. We're going to learn how to coordinate the project plans you've developed so that every activity gets the amount of time it requires. And we're going to learn how to quickly evaluate the requests made for your time so that you can either fit them in or tactfully decline them. We're doing this because as a manager of projects, you owe it to everyone who depends on you or works with you to be a masterful manager of time and the work that fills it.

The knowledge and skills you'll need to effectively manage your time are simple. In fact, the information you'll need to become an effective manager of time is almost trivial; if you don't know it already, you could quickly figure it out. And the skills required to schedule and protect your time aren't mysterious or complicated. Consistently practicing good time-management skills may be simple, but it isn't easy. To turn time-management theory into reality involves more than just learning how to be more efficient and more effective; it requires replacing a few ingrained inefficient habits with new ones. Like healthy eating and exercise, dieting, sobriety, and smokelessness, the hard part of time management isn't knowing what to do, it's doing it. Simple; not easy but quite possible. And, really, isn't it about time you took control of the time of your life?

If efficient, effective, and relatively simple habits are the cornerstone of productivity, how is it that a wonderful person like you ended up struggling to get things done? The answer probably begins in your childhood. Your parents tried to instill the habits of neatness ("Clean your room now, and don't come out till it's done!"), hard work ("No TV till your homework's done!"), and cleanliness ("Go right back in there and wash behind your ears!"). But they never said, "OK, now bring out your to-do list, your weekly schedule, and your priority list so we can go over it." And with few exceptions, your years of formal education were full of structure, schedules, and deadlines that other people imposed on you. School (and employment) teach people how to work, but they don't always teach people how to plan, schedule, prioritize, and manage. The emphasis isn't on balance and efficiency; it's on delivering by the deadline. As a result, "good" students and "good" workers often become sprinters: roaring toward a deadline, making it, stopping to recuperate, and then beginning the dead run again. And like many sprinters, people with a strong work ethic and marginal time-management skills often end up injuring themselves with coronaries, burnout, and/or ulcers. But enough "why"; let's get to the "what" and "how."

Core Time-Management Concepts, Skills, and Attitudes

Priority

Nothing, by itself, has a high priority or a low priority. Priority is a relative thing. For example, while you may think that leaving a burning building must be the highest priority, if you have a lit stick of dynamite duct-taped to your leg, exiting probably slips to number 2. Project managers must be prepared to assess the impact and time demands of a project element, compare that information to other tasks and milestones, and make priority decisions in project schedules and on-the-fly if they expect to be doing the right thing at the right time for the right duration. However, for all the airplay the word "priority" gets, it is often misunderstood.

The priority of a task or outcome is determined by two potentially conflicting components: *importance* and *urgency*. According to *Webster's New World Dictionary*, *important* is defined as "meaning a great deal," which gives us a good clue to how "important" figures into priority. Importance is measured in amounts. Companies and people invest a great deal of time, money, and other resources in important outcomes. The more important the outcome, the more they invest. The consequences for failure also increase in line with increasing importance; the more important an outcome is, the more you'll pay if you fail to produce it. So, when you prioritize a very important task or its outcome, you need to give it the amount of time required to complete it, right up to all the time it needs (which could be months or minutes).

Urgent, according to *Webster,* is defined as "calling for haste, immediate action," and is measured in terms speed, intensity, and focus. A deadline (that point beyond which results become valueless) is set for the delivery of products or services. The closer you get to the deadline without starting the task, the faster and more single-mindedly you must work to stay alive. For example, if your project plan indicates that the only way you can meet a critical path milestone deadline is to start today and work sixteen hours each day, it has high urgency. On the other hand, if the same important outcome will sit on a shelf until others have the necessary equipment to use it, your important task has low urgency. The smaller the difference between the amount of time needed to produce an outcome and the time available to produce that outcome, the more speed, intensity, and focus you must apply to materialize the outcome.

Use the matrix in Figure 5-1 to apply the concepts of priority and urgency to your project management activities, your normal work duties, and the requests made by others.

Most people single-mindedly devote their days to A's (the tasks that produce urgent and important outcomes). As a result,

Figure 5-1. Matrix used to apply concepts of priority and urgency to project management activities.

	Important	Unimportant
Urgent	"A" Priority	Time Bandit
Not Urgent	"B" Priority	Goof-off

many people run into trouble because they fail to promote B's (important but not yet urgent) into A's soon enough. The desire to keep working a task until the result is absolutely perfect, the dread disease procrastination, impromptu meetings that suck otherwise productive hours out of your day, and a dozen other factors can work to keep you from promoting a B task to an A soon enough. The result: A back-burner B catapults into a precardiac A. What can you do? After taming some of the time-eating gremlins mentioned above, try sampling your B tasks for an hour or so well before you think they should regularly appear on your daily work schedule. By taking sixty minutes to preview the scope, complexity, and eventual impact of a task, you'll cut way down on the thrills of tardy task promotion.

More often than not, time is lost to unimportant but urgent time demands that are brought to you by others. Beware the coworker who runs into your office with his eyes bugged and the vein across his forehead throbbing. He may be a time bandit who, wearing the disguise of urgency, steals your time with unimportant tasks. You can see from your coworker's obvious vital signs that he has something urgent going on, but you must find out if it's also important enough to you and/or the company to invest time in. Avoid any tendency to empathize with his urgent neediness and apply the following five-step analysis and action formula.

1. Clarify the coworker's needs ("Let's take a second to find out exactly what I can do for you").
2. Determine the importance of his or her request ("Tell me what will happen if you don't make the deadline").
3. Compare the request with what you have scheduled ("Pardon me while I check my scheduler").
4. Cooperate as much as you can ("I can give you thirty minutes starting right now. Would that be enough?").
5. Circumnavigate this time sinkhole ("I sure would like to help you pardner, but my schedule for today is full up. Sorry 'bout that").

We'll return to protecting our time later in the chapter.

Let's be honest; everyone needs to spend some time on activities that are neither important nor urgent. Hardworking humans need to take a little time to let their brain muscle relax occasionally. A little casual conversation, a hike to the coffee machine, or some gratuitous office straightening won't kill your productivity. Just keep it short and to yourself. More time and goodwill are lost by marching into someone else's day than you would imagine, so unless someone actively invites you to do tag-team brain recharging, recharge alone.

Goals and Milestones

In Chapter 3 we addressed the subject of how goals and milestones were used, but we didn't look carefully enough at what they were. Because they are a language convention designed to ensure the communication of a very specific outcome, it is only right that we examine them more closely.

For most people, goal writing is right up there with tooth flossing: a boring, awkward activity that is supposed to be good for you but that yields little or no apparent results. There are good reasons why so many people cringe when the topic of goal writing arises (the annual goal-writing/performance evaluation ritual, for example), but the truth of the matter is that most fabulously successful people who didn't have good looks, huge brains, or a rich uncle to fall back on use goals to target what they want out of life.

For project managers, however, goals and the milestones that show you the way to goals are absolutely essential to success and sanity. While doing project management tasks, well-written goals help you focus every participant's attention on the mutual outcome. And well-written milestones take the guesswork out of what participants must complete at specific points during the life of the project to stay on track. And while you do your normal work tasks, goals and milestones can add a similar clarity to your work, allowing you to make important priority decisions with confidence.

Project and normal work goals are written on paper (rather than carved in granite) because as needs, wants, possibilities, priorities, and resources shift, you can expect to rewrite goals and milestones to clarify and communicate the changes. But like many things in life, to keep goal writing from being just an exercise, you must learn how to do it right.

How to Make Sure Your Goals Are Wonderful

1. *Think about/picture the outcome you need and want.* Goal writing begins in your head, not on paper. Spend some time pondering what the final outcome will look like, work like, feel like, and do. Don't pick up a pen until you can close your eyes and see the outcome you will describe in your goal.

2. *Write and rewrite your goal(s).* You don't have a goal until it is written down; so-called goals you keep in your head are really "gonna do" intentions ("I'm gonna lose weight when I get around to it"). The purpose of goals is to express exactly what you want to accomplish. If you don't write them down, your goals won't be exact and you will be much less likely to make steady progress toward them. Since it is a *crime* to work without clear goals and an even bigger *crime* to lead a project without goals, Figure 5-2 uses "crime" as a memory cue to help you write great goals every time.

There is no good writing, only good rewriting. Don't try to get it absolutely right the first time. Just capture the idea, then refine it over and over until you're satisfied (or too tired to do it again).

3. *Show others your goals and ask questions.* Communication happens only when a listener or reader understands what you're trying to express. That means that your goal doesn't communicate your targeted outcome until other people can read it and tell you exactly what you're trying to produce. If any confusion between your vision of the outcome and their understanding of it exists after they read the goal, you can and should improve on it. To find out if your goal is really communicating, ask quesions like:

- *"What am I trying to accomplish?"* If the answer leads you to suspect that the reader has somehow looked into your head and examined your three-dimensional vision of the outcome, your goal is clear and measurable.

Figure 5-2. Memory cue used to write goals.

C lear—Can two or more people who have read your goal fully agree on the look, feel, function, and smell of the outcome, or is there room for "interpretation"?

R easonable—Is the goal challenging but possible to accomplish?

I mportant—Does the goal describe an outcome your company really needs and that, in your job, you should target?

M easurable—Does the goal include a way to accurately gauge whether the outcome is complete, half done, or somewhere in between?

E xpiration-Dated—Exactly when must you either celebrate completion or start making excuses?

- *"Compared to other activities and outcomes, how important is this?"* With project goals and milestones, you probably have a good idea of importance at this point. But with your nonproject duties and, occasionally during project plan revisions, this question will help you plan and schedule.
- *"Do you think it's possible to accomplish this goal in the time available without ditching other activities?"* If this is the top priority outcome of a particular project phase and/or if you don't have to shortchange other important milestones to accomplish it, your goal is reasonable. Otherwise, some adjusting might be in order.
- *"Do you have any suggestions for adjusting this goal?* If the goal affects others, make sure you show it to them, ask

them all the questions listed above, and adjust the goal if for no other reason than to promote their buy-in.

Don't zip by this reality check. The easiest person for you to kid is yourself, so let someone you trust and respect give you good information about your goals. Not only will they help you improve them; the fact that they know you've set goals will help you stay on course toward their accomplishment.

How to Select and Use a Daily Planner

As difficult as it is to believe, some project managers don't use a planner at all and others don't use planners well. If you fall into either of these categories and you want to be an effective project manager, prepare for a change. It is virtually impossible to manage projects and your normal work efficiently and effectively if you don't carry and make the most out of some sort of planner.

The most frequently used planners are attractive and expensive books of varying size that people use as a memory supplement, which is the absolute minimum value one can get out of them without losing them altogether. Most daily planner carriers capture the date of the meeting they're supposed to attend next month or make a note about the report they're supposed to submit on a particular day so they won't forget it. This function could be more economically served with Post-its attached to computers and desks. Some planner carriers capture milestone dates too, which is better but doesn't do much to help you plan or protect the time needed to achieve the milestone. To get the maximum yield from a planner, you must load the components of your individual work plans and your project plans into them and use the plan schedules to drive your day- and your time-use decisions. While your project chart is an effective way to communicate the planned course of work and outcomes, you may have several projects going on at the same time and almost surely have additional, nonproject work to do. That's why a planner will serve as the organizational core of your projects, your work, and your overall productivity. Let's start learning how to use one by making sure you have or get a good one.

Tips for People Who Need to Buy a Daily Planner

Planners come in three types: book, computer, and electronic handheld gizmo. There are many varieties of each type with many features to choose from. Book-type planners come in a wide range of shapes, sizes, weights, costs, and degrees of comprehensiveness. Software packages for computers and handheld electronic planners also come in several shapes and memory sizes, with more hitting the market every day.

Several large companies sell book-type planners. Most offer a few hours of training (either in person for large group purchases or via tape recordings for individuals) and a variety of sizes to choose from, ranging from the relatively simple and small to multiple cross-reference weight-lifter specials. Professionally researched and executed, these book-type planners are uniformly well done and, with their range of choices, would certainly satisfy your needs.

If you like electronic gadgets and aren't afraid of battery failure, the handheld electronic planners can be helpful. Some will link with computers to upload and download information, and some have screens large enough to show an entire month's schedule. As very small portable computers continue evolving toward lower costs and greater power, the days of high-touch/low-tech planner books are numbered. Since already existing electronic planners have the same features you can get from a book-type planner, the real question is not if you will use an electronic planner but when to make the transition. If handheld planners interest you but you're unsure, find someone who uses one and ask about their experience. Chances are they'll either sing its praises or offer you a bargain price on their used one.

Computer-based planner software programs are usually very powerful, flexible, and easy to work with and have alarms to buzz at you when it's time to do something. Portability is their Achilles' heel. If you need to check or revise your schedule when you are away from your screen, you'll be forced to backpedal until you can get to your computer. If you spend most of your time at your desktop and/or have your laptop up and running continuously, a computerized planner is a good choice for you.

Otherwise, consider a book-type planner or a handheld electronic planner that can communicate with your computer.

The best planner for you is the most comprehensive one that you will consistently use. The trouble with breaking into planner use is that well-intentioned people just like you buy their first planner with great enthusiasm and marginal habits. They buy planners only to find them, months later, lurking in the back of closets, stuffed in desk drawers, or littering their cars (check under the seats). After the first spurt of good intentions is exhausted, far too many externally structured, personally disorganized, and well-intentioned people stop using their planners and revert to their chaotic habits. There is hope, however. Here's one way to find a book-type planner that is well suited for you.

Go to an office-supply superstore. (Bookstores typically don't stock planners, and small office-supply stores charge high prices.) Rummage through their choices, looking for one that gives you enough space to note what you'll be doing in any given hour, suits your travel needs (if you don't leave your work area often, you can get a bigger one, but if you travel around much, you should consider a less bulky variety), and is cheap. Buy it and dedicate yourself to using it (see "Loading Your Planner" and "Working Your Schedule," below). If this planner works well for you, great. And if it doesn't, figure out whether your bad habits got the best of you or if you need a better-suited planner. If you need something different in a planner—for example, a different-size planner, one that allows you to see an entire week at a time, or one that has a more impressive cover— chalk up your first choice to experience and use what you've learned to purchase a second.

Loading Your Planner: Nonproject Work and Outcomes

1. A number-two pencil with a sharp point is an excellent choice to enter all the nonproject events you know about, such as meetings, presentations, vacations, and other "I've got to be somewhere doing something on this date" kind of things. Block out the planner entry from start to finish with either specific

notes to yourself about the event and, if space remains, with a big X.

2. Enter any repetitive tasks at the time(s) they must be done. These are tasks that don't have an "it's over" outcome; they simply require doing every day. For example, you may set aside twenty minutes per day, starting at 10 A.M., to retrieve and respond to your mail.

3. List on a sheet of paper every normal work-duty outcome you must complete and the date it must be finished.

4. For each outcome you've listed, describe milestones (intermediate outcomes just like the ones you've already worked with for your project plan).

5. Enter all the outcomes and milestones on their due dates from the final outcome deadline backwards to today.

6. After entering each outcome/milestone sequence, work forward from today, scheduling enough work time so you can produce the milestones and outcomes on time. Keep these timing tips in mind as you schedule your days:

Timing Tips

a. *Schedule tasks that require laserlike focus when your level of concentration is greatest.* Consider whether you are a morning person or someone who needs a coffee IV to register a heartbeat before noon.

b. *If you normally make several outgoing calls a day as part of your job, try to make most of them as early in the day as possible.* You are more likely to reach people early in the day and, if you leave a message on their machine, you're more likely to get a return call that day.

c. *Be prepared to use voice mail correctly.* Prepare a detailed message before you dial. That way, people can give you an answer on your voice mail without interrupting you later.

7. Review your planner for schedule-overload. If, after loading your scheduler with all your normal work, deadlines, meetings, vacations, etc., you must work six days a week and

ten hours each day to get the work out, turn your pencil around and pick up the phone. If your nonproject work plans are already at overload, you will not only fail to meet your goals and be unable to handle the inevitable intrusions and emergencies, you will have no hope of successfully managing a project. Do whatever you need to do to adjust deadlines, jettison events, or offload some responsibilities. Work at thinning your normal work schedule until there is enough time to schedule project management activities.

Loading Your Planner: Project Management Duties

With the nonproject part of your work loaded in your planner, you're ready to plug in the tasks, deadlines, review meetings, and all other essential project management activities and outcomes. If you're thinking of using the project chart you recently developed, don't. You must integrate the project schedule with management activities that don't appear on the chart (e.g., review meetings), with other projects you're managing and with your nonproject activities and outcomes. At the core of every plan and schedule are coordination and balance. Putting everything in one place allows you to coordinate your schedule and balance your priorities. So, whip out your project chart and your planner, and let's load your project into your book-type planner by the numbers:

1. Flip forward to the project deadline. Pencil in a block of time big enough for a meeting and presentation on that day. Using your notes from the initial review meeting you had with your prime mover, pencil in the periodic reviews' meeting dates.

2. If you're working with one or more collaborators, transfer their scheduled project-work start dates and their milestone deadlines from the project chart to your planner. A day or more before each start date, note in your planner to gently remind/ confirm key collaborators ("Joe, I just thought I'd call before you start on the credit data processing task to see if there is anything I need to do to make sure you've got everything you need to start on the 12th"). You may not need to do this with every collaborator, but rookies and the very busy should get a wake-up

call. You may also want to include a reminder to tactfully back-stop them shortly before completion dates ("Joe, I'm looking forward to our credit data summary meeting next week and was wondering if there was anything I could do in the way of preparation"). Of course, your coworkers are capable, diligent people who don't need you badgering them. But if you make a practice of blind faith, someone will eventually drop the ball and blow your project schedule.

3. Take a moment to reflect on your personal work preferences before taking the next step, which is scheduling your project work time. Because of our individual metabolisms, our past work habits, our eating and sleeping patterns, and several other factors, every moment of every day is not created equal. Some times (like the early hours for "morning people") are well suited for high levels of energy and concentration, and other times (like after lunch) are well suited for activities that require less focus. As you schedule your day, try to match each activity of the day with the thinking resources you can bring to it. If you concentrate best in the morning and the activity of the day is writing, schedule writing time in the A.M. If an informal update is the activity of the day, consider taking the person you need to talk with to lunch. But whatever you do, don't abandon a balanced schedule for a nearsighted to-do list.

4. Schedule time to (1) review milestones on the date they are to occur, (2) monitor rookie work activities, and (3) prepare for periodic review meetings. Confirming the quality and timeliness of outcomes that collaborators hand off to each other guards against handoff fumbles (and is a big part of why you are allowed to call yourself the project leader). Gathering information about a rookie's progress and stepping in before it stalls can save you and the rookie from days of frustration and catch-up.

Setting aside time to prepare for oral or written progress reviews keeps prime movers current while it gives you an opportunity to confirm and, if needed, rekindle their support.

5. Now, repeat steps 1–4 for every other project you're leading.

6. Do an "Am I overloaded?" reality check to see if you have committed yourself to too many twelve-hour days. As be-

fore, do whatever you need to do to adjust deadlines or offload some of your responsibilities. If that doesn't work, try shaving some time from project work blocks—remove whiskers but don't peel off the skin—or moving a couple of hours of work from an overloaded day to a nearby underloaded one. Try to recruit another project collaborator. Ask your boss for a get-out-of-meeting-free card for regular, sort-of-important meetings. Delegate some of your nonproject work. Volunteer for a cloning experiment.

7. Finally, if you find that you can't get it all done in the goal deadline times available, even after applying a reasonable extra effort, talk to a project prime mover and ask to push back a deadline. With your schedule and adjustment efforts in hand, you should be pretty persuasive. When you're finished with this, you should have every important activity and outcome entered into your planner in a way that has the potential for keeping them from becoming unreasonably urgent.

Working Your Schedule

Now that the easy part is done, you can turn your attention to working the schedule. Practically anyone can schedule their work into some sort of time matrix. But a well-organized schedule, like a well-organized budget, doesn't save you anything if you don't follow it carefully. Fred Brooks, a computer designer for IBM, is credited with saying, "How does a project get to be a year behind schedule? One day at a time." In addition to your habitual inefficiencies, accept the fact that the intrusions of co-workers, unexpected technical problems, delays caused by others, and underestimates of the effort needed to accomplish an event can put you far enough behind so that meeting milestones becomes impossible. In this section, we'll consider some ways to stay on track.

Sunday Night

Spend thirty to sixty minutes looking through your planner; survey the status of every ongoing project as of the end of last week and review the week to come. As you look through your project chart(s) and plans, ask yourself:

1. "Are there any milestones during the week?"
2. "Is a participant scheduled to start a task or complete a milestone?"
3. "Is there a particularly difficult aspect of the project coming up?"
4. "Am I significantly behind or ahead of schedule?"

Make notes detailing your answers: "Mktg Milestone on the 12th," "G. Jones starts data analysis on 3rd," etc.

Next, ask yourself, "What must I accomplish this week?" After looking up the easy ones (milestones and deadlines), focus on the work that isn't anchored to a near-term milestone.

How much progress should you make this week in order to stay on schedule with milestones or deadlines that are coming up in two weeks or a month? Ask yourself, "Have I learned anything that inclines me to adjust the project schedule?" Add these longer-range musings of what must be accomplished by Friday to the notes you took earlier. After looking at this list, consider just how pinched you'll be for time. If you need to find five or six hours, now is the time to find them. Make any necessary adjustments to the week's schedule, giving particular emphasis to Monday.

Daily

Make a habit of starting each day by opening your planner and sticking to the schedule. If necessary, plan adjustments for afternoon activities during lunch. The last thing you should do before leaving work in the afternoon is review your progress during the day and make necessary adjustments for tomorrow.

Wednesday Afternoon

Do a mini-version of your Sunday night review. You've still got two days left to make your planned progress, so take thirty minutes or so to decide what it will take to finish on plan and on schedule.

Protecting Your Schedule

Let's say that instead of loading a planner and working a schedule, you've decided to load a financial plan into a budget book and to work that budget. You want to make the best use of your money, so you make decisions about what you're going to buy and, consequently, what you're not going to buy. With your brand-new budget book sitting next to you, your brother-in-law (or neighbor or coworker) walks in, removes your wallet, and starts helping himself to some cash. Later, someone else arrives and starts writing checks to herself, which you sign! At 10 A.M. you get up and go to a meeting, but within minutes, the meeting leader walks over to you and starts pulling off your rings and unclasping your gold necklace. No problem, right? *Wrong!*

We have no problem stopping people who would take our valuables, because the rules about and against stealing money and jewels are clear. But when it comes to stealing the nonrenewable resource called time, we tend to adopt the Scarlett O'Hara philosophy, "Tomorrow is another day!" Sure it is; another day toward deadline disaster. If you don't protect your time, as it appears in your schedule, you're better off flying the project by the seat of your pants. At least that way, you won't squander the time you would have invested in developing a plan.

So what are you, the project leader, to do? Ruthlessly protect your schedule and your plan with preemptive interruption repellent, with priority-gauging probes, and with schedule-driven responses.

Preemptive Interruption Repellent

Without traffic signals, cars would be crashing into each other all the time with occasionally fatal results. In this era of cubicles and open office architecture, people in the recharge mode are constantly crashing into folks who are diligently working, and the results are productivity-sapping. The problem lies with the absence of universally recognized traffic signals. For many, the rule is that if you can see someone, you can talk to him (or her). And when you do, that deeply absorbed person loses the dozen or so thoughts he's keeping straight in his head. Even if he effectively brushes you off, it takes several (like about twelve) minutes to get back into the train of thought. Take several of those hits in a day and you can easily burn an hour or more. You need a traffic signal.

Using a traffic signal of some sort (a closed door, an I'M BUSY NOW sign, or yellow crime-scene tape across your cubical portal) is only half the answer. Some people will require a little training before they respond to your signal in the desired way. For example, when Bruce the Interrupter ignores your stop sign and launches into his well-known "How ya doin'" opening to the all too familiar twenty-minute "What I did on my weekend" review, immediately stand and cut him off. Walk toward him with a smile and say something like:

> ***Project Manager:*** Bruce, you sure would be a breath of fresh air if I had time to breathe. [*Talking right through his attempt to gain control of the conversation, you continue:*] You know, I'm so swamped with work that I've had to resort to closing my door so I can really focus in on . . . [*glance at your watch and quietly exclaim a quick, surprised:*] Ouuuu—my twelve-thirty deadline! Could you do this for me, Bruce: For the next couple of weeks, let me come over and visit you when I can afford to come up for a breather? I hate to lock myself away like

this, but if I don't, I'll never finish this project on time.
OK?

Does Bruce know you've told him to buzz off and to observe
your closed door? Yes. Are his feelings hurt? Probably not. The
trick is to word the buzz-off message so it conveys some degree
of respect. If Bruce leaves with his face intact, he'll still remain
an acquaintance but he'll think twice or more before barging
into your office.

Priority-Gauging Probes

Some interruptions come with a bona fide request for help
attached. As we observed earlier, the first challenge is to find out
how urgent and important these requests are compared to the
work you have scheduled. Don't base your estimate of the priority of these interruptions on the bugged-out eyes and pulsing
veins of the requester. Certainly, their need is urgent, but urgency alone does not give something a high priority. Their need
must be more urgent and more important than what you have
scheduled. Clarify the level of importance and urgency with
these carefully worded probes:

"What do you need my help to accomplish?"

"Whom are you doing this for?"

"What would happen if I couldn't help you right now/this
morning/today/at all?"

"Would X minutes of my help be enough?"

The suggestion to question interrupters makes more than a few
people nervous. They worry that "I won't be viewed as a team
player" or "If I don't help them, they won't help me when I need
it" or "When my boss says 'jump,' I don't probe, I jump!" Well,
how nervous do blown deadlines make you? How nervous are
you when you must work late into the night because someone
squandered hours of your day? How nervous does the prospect
of a "he's never around"–based divorce make you? Don't get

yourself fired by trying to probe a stressed-out boss while you're wearing an understanding smile on your face. But don't roll over just because someone asks you to. Ask questions that allow you to spend your time knowledgeably and productively!

Schedule-Driven Responses

Learn to say no when your task is more urgent and important than the requester's. Be suitably sorry and helpful, but say no. If the request is in fact important and somewhat urgent, find a block of time assigned to a less urgent task in your schedule and offer to help ("I could help you for an hour this afternoon starting at 2 P.M.; how does that sound?"). And if the request is both important and more urgent than what you're working on at the time, help immediately, but indicate exactly how long you can assist ("I can help for the next hour, if that makes sense to you").

Once you commit your goals and plans to a schedule, the realization of your potential productivity gains depends on working and protecting that schedule. It will feel peculiar for a while, but if you discipline yourself to living by a schedule, you'll begin to see some real changes in the results you can manage out of others and out of yourself. As you reap the productivity gains that come from your investment in planning and goal setting, the self-discipline that you had to force will transform into habits that you wouldn't consider relinquishing.

Chapter 6

Influencing Participants

Respect the man and he will do more.

> —Red Barber, Sportscaster and Commentator

The only way I can get you to do anything is by giving you what you want.

> —Dale Carnegie

Poetry in motion. Yes, that was how Jack's software update project was going. For that matter, all his work was going like poetry in motion. Every morning he would review the schedule for his day and begin work. Intrusions would present themselves, but now they were assessed, prioritized, and blended into his schedule. At the end of each day, work that wasn't completed was reviewed and rescheduled. At midweek, Jack reviewed his progress and made adjustments to his schedule. On Fridays, he devoted a couple of hours to updating and adjusting his schedule for the upcoming week. Jack's motivation was rising about as fast as his level of productivity, which were both trending toward new highs. Then he called Phil, the project participant responsible for updating parts of the inventory software.

"I've got bad news, my friend," Jack heard on the phone, but he could have sworn that Phil's voice sounded like a finely tuned car running headlong into a brick wall. "I know I'm supposed to test and debug your inventory control prototype this week, but I just took on a major new task that has to be done yesterday. Working twelve-hour days, I won't be done until next month. Sorry, pal, but you're just going to have to wait.''

This can happen to any project at any time. People make commitments that they cannot or will not keep. Your best-laid plans go astray not because you don't work hard to keep them on track but because other people blindside you with bad news just at the moment you need them most. If you think keeping a project on schedule when you're the only one involved can be frustrating, try coordinating other people. The phrase "Hurry up and wait" may have been coined in the military, but when people from a range of groups and departments must interlock schedules, even well-planned projects sometimes come to a screeching halt. So what's a project manager to do?

The Psychology and Strategy of Influence/Persuasion

People usually try to influence others by explaining a situation as they see it and then asking for what they want. Or, even less productively, they will explain a situation and then wait for the other person to make an offer of assistance. While these approaches may seem logical, they don't work well or frequently. The "logical approach" to influencing becomes even less effective when the person you are trying to influence balks. It's at this point that most logical influencers shift into the debate mode, arguing the merits of their point. Positions are taken, decisions are solidified, and the logical influencer wipes out any hope s/he had of getting what s/he wanted. Getting people to do what they aren't naturally inclined to do requires more than conveying facts; it requires an understanding of human nature and motivation. In this chapter, we'll apply some of the information that has been accumulated about human nature and various influencing techniques to situations where you, as a project manager, must influence participants and stakeholders. But before we start influencing fickle collaboraters, let's lay a persuasion skill foundation.

The Psychology of Influence: Hidden Persuaders

Psychology, the study of behavior, and salesmanship, the practice of influence for profit, have accumulated considerable practical information about both influence and persuasion. Robert Cialdini, a social psychologist and the author of *Influence,* identifies several subtle principles of persuasion that apply to almost all human beings and which are described below. If you engage in these hidden persuaders from the beginning, you'll be significantly less likely to end up with Jack's dilemma.

Reciprocation

Most people have a strong desire to return favors, pay back debts, and give things to people who have given things to them. Time, kindness, money, presents, or practically any other identifiable thing that one person can give to another creates a social pressure on the receiver to reciprocate. Recall the feeling you had when you got an unexpected present from someone who wasn't on your shopping list.

As a project manager, look for opportunities to make a reciprocation link between yourself and participants, stakeholders, and the prime mover. Make a habit of being generous with your time, advice, and other assets. Look for opportunities to be thoughtful to others, particularly if you must rely on them. Of course, give without expecting things in return and don't let your thoughtfulness and generousity compromise your devotion to time-management practices. Your habit of giving time and effort will be repaid by participants who are more inclined to prioritize your project when you need them to than to park it in favor of a competing project.

Commitment and Consistency

When you received a specific commitment from participants and the prime mover, you significantly increased their inclination to behave in ways that are consistent with that commitment. The more specific the commitment and the more people it is made in front of, the more consistent a person is likely to be about it. From salespeople "closing" the sale by asking for a specific commitment to well-attended marriage ceremonies in which the minister asks "Do you take this . . . ," there are many examples of people staying on a particular course because they made a commitment to it.

Effective project managers ask for commitments. Ask for someone's commitment to help clearly and directly ("John, will you spend all day Thursday and Friday of next week working with me on this project?"). Once a person makes a specific commitment, particularly in a meeting, send a confirmation message clearly stating the nature of the commitment. If there is more than a week between the commitment and the action, send a reminder shortly before the participant is scheduled to help ("Just a short note to thank you in advance for your help next Tuesday on the budgeting process").

Social Proof

People are strongly inclined to act like people they view as peers or as powerful. The more consistent the peer/powerful person's behavior is, the more likely it is that associates will act in the same way. This should not be surprising when you consider that humans learn most of their behavior from viewing and duplicating the actions of parents and other people they are close to. From herds of cloned teenage "rebels" to the "group think" mentality of some organizations, our tendency to look to the behavior of others for guidance about our own behavior is commonplace. Recall the last unfamiliar social situation you were in (fancy restaurant, opera, ethnic wedding reception, etc.). How did you decide what to do? If you watched everyone around you and tried to blend in, you had firsthand experience with social proof.

As the project manager, you may have to mediate social proof for participants who aren't able to observe each other often. Let project participants know who the prime movers are, who else is working on the project, and who is waiting for its results. If you prepare written progress reviews for a prime mover, consider distributing them to the other stakeholders who are interested and/or involved in the project. Whenever prudently possible, make sure that key collaborators know the task is important and that coworkers are counting on them.

Liking

Being able to attract the attention of others is an important component of influence. All things being equal, the well-groomed, upbeat, smiling, warm, thoughtful person is able to get more of what s/he wants from others than the messy, unhappy, frowning, distant, self-absorbed person. If you don't believe it, just look around you for a while. One of the most consistent aspects of successful salespeople, who are professional influencers by definition, is their habitually upbeat attitude and their consistent attention to dress and grooming. Dale Carnegie's classic, *How to Win Friends and Influence People,* examines many of the small but all-important habits that affect other people's liking reactions and, as such, is a good primer on the art of being liked.

Don't fall into the bad habit of "letting your hair down" with project participants or coworkers generally. When you let crabbiness, self-pity, cynicism, stress-out, or anger into your actions or reactions, you become less attractive and less influential. Just because people listen to you when you complain doesn't mean they like to hear it or like being around people who do it. Read Carnegie's book and take it to heart. Smile at people with your face and your voice. Make a habit of looking for positive features you can compliment others about. And when anyone shows interest in or makes a contribution to your project, be attentive and thankful.

Scarcity

People are much more likely to make a decision and take action if they believe that their window of opportunity is closing. From centuries-old proverbs like "He who hesitates is lost" to retail marketing's ONE-DAY-ONLY SALE, the inertia of people to make decisions can be overcome by focusing on the limited amount of time that remains before the opportunity to make any decisions will disappear.

The secret to effectively applying the principle of scarcity is to use it sparingly. Emphasize the urgency to take action or make a decision only when the need is actually urgent. If you ask for immediate help when the need isn't really urgent, people will catch on and slow down. But if you use your ruthless command of time-management practices to remain as proactive as possible, your urgent requests for immediate help will carry much more weight.

The Tactics of Persuasion

The hidden persuaders described above are important tools for project managers to use as they forge compliant relationships. Without asking for any action, doing things that promote reciprocation and that engage social proof will incline participants and stakeholders to listen and say yes when a request is necessary. When circumstances require that you ask for action or a decision, you can increase your likelihood of a yes even more by using the time-honored tactics that are commonplace to professional salespeople.

Earning the Right

Most of the power to influence others comes from information you obtain from them. In order to gather influential information, you must first earn the right to ask questions in a way that avoids triggering resistance and promotes a willingness to talk candidly:

> *Project Manager:* Harold, I'm leading a project designed to improve the quality of our products at this facility. We are currently under way and hope to finish by the 15th of next month. The reason I'm here today is that we've run into a snag with packaging vendors' providing us with information. Because you have been the person who is most involved with vendor relations and with authorizing their invoices, I've come to you for your insight and suggestions about how I can get them to be more revealing.

Determining Priorities and Objections

Before actively trying to influence someone, an effective persuader must find out as much as possible about the other person's wants, needs, misgivings, misunderstandings, and priorities. Xerox studied the behavior of thousands of its sales-people and found that effective influencers talk 30 percent of the time and listen 70 percent. In order to get someone you want to influence to talk that much, you'll have to spend most of your 30 percent asking questions that will encourage the person being influenced to reveal his or her priorities (what s/he wants) and his or her objections (what s/he doesn't want).

> "Harold, tell me what you've heard about the quality improvement project, if anything?"

> "Can you foresee any value to the company or to your department from adjusting the way our vendors ship materials to us?"

> "Are there problems that you think might arise from changing the shipping schedule and standards with packaging vendors?"

Turning the Corner: The Moment of Truth

Sometimes, the best thing to do once you've got all the facts is to thank the person for their time, congratulate them on the good work they are doing and that they intend to continue doing (without being interrupted by your request for help), and leave. If the information you've gathered clearly indicates that an intruding task is a higher priority than their commitment to your project, you will only waste everyone's time by trying to persuade them to change their priorities. On the other hand, if you believe that you can convince the person that it is better to change their mind, you want to let them know that you've turned the corner from gathering information to giving it. Turning the corner usually comes in the form of an "if-then" question like the ones below:

> *Project Manager:* Thank you for being so candid and comprehensive about the new inventory system. You've provided me with a lot of background information about your department that I wasn't aware of. If I can show you how splitting Phil's time between the inventory and shipment scheduling tasks will allow both

tasks to move forward on schedule, then would you be willing to give me two or three hours of his time each day for the next week?"

[*or*] I certainly understand the needs and priority of your group's credit reporting work better now that you've explained it to me. Listening to what you've said, I think there might be a mutually beneficial way of keeping your group's work and my project on schedule, but you'll have to be the final judge. If I can develop a schedule that allows Florence to work on my project only when she would otherwise be waiting for input from your field personnel, then would you be willing to give it a try for a week?

Presenting Their Case

Yes, *their* case, not yours. People aren't influenced by what you want; they're influenced by what they want. So take the information you gathered earlier and, priority by priority, explain why changing their mind will produce a better course of action than the one they are on presently. And, if you have any doubt at all about the person's comprehension or agreement, probe to make sure they understood and agreed with you ("Can you see how this downtime approach to scheduling Florence's time would maximize her productivity, allow your group to stay on schedule, and let me keep my project commitments?").

Close

After presenting each point in their case, you'll be ready to ask for a decision. Here are several paths you can take to yes:

"So, can we start splitting Florence's time starting tomorrow, or would you like to begin Monday?"

"Wouldn't you agree that splitting Florence's time makes a lot of sense?"

"Would you like to tell Florence about the new arrangement, or should I?"

Don't wait for the person being influenced to change their mind by themselves; help them by asking.

The Paths and Politics of Influencing Reluctant Participants

If an important participant bails out just when s/he's needed on a task, some people conclude that there's nothing they can do but plead a little and wring their hands. Nothing could be further from the truth. The decision tree shown in Figure 6-1 describes a number of options and actions available to you. As we go through them, we will apply the tactics of persuasion to the practical realities of everyday work.

Step 1: Fact-Find Priority

For some obscure reason, which you must reveal, a participant has decided that working on your project has a lower priority than doing something else. Working on the competing task must seem more urgent than working on your task; otherwise, the collaborator would simply put off the intruding task until she had honored her commitment to you. But is the intruding task really more urgent and more important? Does it really require the participant's time right now and in the quantities that make it impossible to help you? Because the participant is completely up to speed on the project and the situation at hand, you can dispense with "earning the right" and go directly to "fact finding."

The probes listed in Figure 6-2 are designed to help you uncover information about the urgency and importance of the intruding task so that you can make comparisons to the tasks required of the participant by your project.

Try not to make the participant feel badgered. Most people, when pushed, start resisting, and that's the last thing you want to trigger. At this point, your objective is to get enough information to (1) assess whether there is any hope of reselling the collaborator on helping you and, if so, (2) gathering enough information to effectively do the reselling.

Figure 6-1. A decision tree.

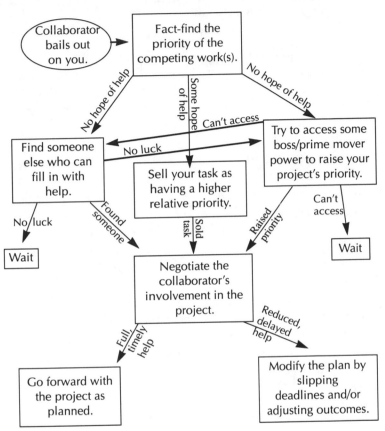

Figure 6-2. Probes used to fact-find priority.

---
1. "Tell me about the new task."
2. "Who else is working on it?"
3. "Who brought this one to you?"
4. "When will you be starting?"
5. "Did you mention our task schedule when you got the new task?"
6. "What would happen if this new task were delayed?

Step 2: Get Some Help

If there is no hope of personally reselling the participant on helping you as planned, you have two options. Your choice of options can affect your future relationship with the collaborator, so
you'll want to give it some thought. The less hazardous choice
is to ask your former participant to help find a replacement for
the project. Your former participant will probably be an informed and enthusiastic resource in selecting a stand-in, since
finding someone to fill in gets him or her off the hook. If you
can't find anyone to fill in, you can either wait until your coworker can fit your project into his or her schedule or you can
or try option 2: accessing enough boss power to regain your collaborator's help. Option 2 is hazardous, so let's take a moment
to consider it.

One of the chief responsibilities of managers is to assign,
compare, calibrate, and adjust priorities. They must make sure
that their direct reports are effective (that they are doing the
right things) and efficient (that they are doing things right).
Many times, a new task can be assigned without considering its
impact on other, ongoing work. By reviewing the impact of an
intruding task on the project you have in process, you help man-
agers/bosses/prime movers make important decisions.

There is another way of looking at this option. By accessing
power in a way that raises the priority of your project task without enlisting the cooperation and involvement of your participant, you are almost sure to reduce their willingness to help
you. If, after a fact-finding meeting with you, the participant gets
a call from their boss telling them to give you the help you need,

your reward will almost surely be some version of malicious compliance. And the version of malicious compliance you're likely to get is called permanent. So consider the following approach:

> *Project Manager:*   Maurice, from what you tell me, this new assignment is important to your boss, Ralph, but may be something that could be delayed long enough for you to help me. Would you have any objection to spending a few minutes with Ralph and me to review your involvement in the new assignment and in our project? I just want to remind Ralph of the project we've got going to see if there's any way he could adjust your invovlement in the new assignment. Would you have any problem with that?

If your participant resists the idea of going to the prime mover, you've got an important decision to make. You can (1) talk to his boss anyway, (2) wait until the original participant becomes available, or (3) try to find a stand-in for your project. Whichever decision you make, you owe the participant the courtesy of saying what you intend to do.

Step 3: Influence Others to Raise Your Task's Priority

At this point in the decision tree, you are either going to influence your original participant to return to his project commitment or you're going to influence the participant's boss to change priorities so the participant can remain involved in the project. If you've decided to attempt a shift from fact finding to selling your task to the original participant, you might turn the corner with an if-then statement like this:

> *Project Manager:*   If I can show you why George's task can wait until Friday, then will you stick to the plan we discussed and start working on the database development task now?

If his answer is "I suppose so" or something similarly encouraging, you can start discussing how the project benefits him, his group, and/or the company. If his answer indicates that he can't or won't prioritize your project work, you might elect to wait, look for a stand-in, or attempt to influence his boss.

Because the priorities and objections of each situation tend to be different, there is no "influence-by-the-numbers" format to follow as you present their case. The example below simply illustrates how one typical Step 3 might go:

Project Manager: When we talked about the new assignment you've been asked to do, you mentioned three reasons why you would have to postpone working on our project: that you had to finish the new assignment by Wednesday of next week, that you didn't know how long it would take to finish it, and that your boss wasn't really involved with our project. If I can show you why starting the new task can wait until tomorrow, will you be willing to consider sticking to the plan we discussed and start working on the database now?"

Participant: I suppose so.

Project Manager: Great! Then let me begin with the issue of your boss's interest in our project. You're right that he didn't initiate the project; I got it from Phil, my boss. But Phil was asked to get this done by Marilyn, who is not only Phil's boss but also your boss's boss. As I understand it, Marilyn wants our project completed by Thursday of next week because she has to spend a day with it before presenting it to a group of buyers in Cleveland. That meeting is set and if I can't deliver on time, I'm going to have to do some tall explaining. So, while your boss isn't directly involved in this project, if it doesn't get done by Thursday, I think there's a good chance he will become involved. What do you think?

Participant: Well, since you put it that way, I can see where my boss would be interested in the project, but remember that the new assignment is also important. If I can't get it done by Wednesday, I'll have problems

as big as the ones you describe for missing your deadline.

Project Manager: I understand. Let's look at the urgency
issue this way. If you decide to go with the new assignment, the chances of missing my project deadline are
100 percent and the chances of missing the new-assign-
ment deadline are basically unknown. If you give me
today to work on our task, the chances of missing my
deadline go down to around zero percent and the
chances of missing your deadline are still unknown.
Given that, doesn't it seem reasonable to ensure at least
one win out of two instead of ensuring one missed
deadline?

Participant [*after a very long pause*]: OK. Get out of here so
I can do my part of our project.

You started by summarizing what you learned in fact finding,
and followed up by turning the corner from fact finding to highlighting benefits and handling objections. If you missed any key
points or if the participant wasn't willing to even entertain being
sold, you would have found out as you tried to turn the corner.
After the participant expressed a willingness to talk, you started
with the most potent point: power-related importance. The point
got your participant's attention, but his sense of urgency to start
the new assignment, not knowing how long it would take to
complete, was still an objection. You overcame it by comparing
the benefits of ensuring one success out of two versus ensuring
one disaster out of two. Seeing the relative advantage, the participant decided to put one success in the bank.

If you decide to try influencing the prime mover/boss,
you'll first have to begin at the beginning (see Figure 6-3) by
earning the right to ask probing questions about an intruding
task. When s/he knows why you are asking questions, you can
begin fact finding to gauge and compare the priorities of the
intruding task with the project tasks you're trying to protect. If
s/he seems amenable to discussing an adjustment of the participant's schedule, turn the corner with an if-then question presenting their case and ask for a commitment. Again, each

situation will differ according to the priorities and objections, but the example below will give you a sense of one typical influencing conversation.

> *Project Manager:*   I've got something of a problem that I need your advice and help on. I'm leading an ongoing project to improve product quality and have enlisted Sam's assistance in compiling key data for my final report. When I called him this morning to touch base before his data-handling part of the project begins, he told me that he has a new task that he's got to start immediately. If I could, I'd like to take ten minutes of your time to get some more information, since this new task requirement is going to result in a missed deadline for the quality project Sam and I have been working on. I would try to get a fill-in for Sammy if I could, but unfortunately for me, he's the only person here at the corporate office who is sufficiently familiar with the project to finish his part by our deadline. Would it be all right if I asked a few questions?
>
> *Sam's Boss:*   Of course; fire away.
>
> *Project Manager:*   As Sam has explained to me, his deadline is four days away. Is there any flexibility in that or would that be the drop-dead date?
>
> *Sam's Boss:*   I'm afraid that we've got to take Sammy's results out to our stores in five days, so we'll need it in four just to review it and make copies. And if we miss that deadline, we won't be able to get this out for another month.
>
> *Project Manager:*   The cost analysis that you've given Sam to complete, as I understand it, involves bringing together some pretty complex databases. Is he the only analyst in the department who can handle the task or is there someone who could either help him or fill in for him?
>
> *Sam's Boss:*   There are certainly people who could handle this job, but I don't feel comfortable letting a less experienced analyst do this. It's got to be right the first time, and I know Sam can do it.

Figure 6-3. Steps used to influence others.

1. *Earn the right.*

   Explain/justify why you're probing for information.

2. *Probe/fact-find.*

   Ask probes and questions that reveal importance (why does something get time and resources?) and urgency (what is the absolute drop-dead date?).

3. *Turn the corner.*

   Ask an "if-then" question that determines whether the target is willing to be influenced and specifies what must be presented to be successful in your influencing attempt.

4. *Present information/solutions.*

   Detail benefits or alternative actions that convince the target that changing or compromising is the best decision.

5. *Ask for a commitment.*

   Just that. When the target indicates that s/he's been convinced, ask for a specific decision.

Project Manager: Would it be possible to streamline this analysis at all so that your basic requirements could be met while still leaving enough time for Sam to apply the single day I need him on our project?

Sam's Boss: I can't really answer that until I see Sam's initial report outline.

Project Manager: If I can show you how Sam's involvement in your task and in my project can be organized so we both successfully meet our deadlines, would you be willing to consider sharing him?

Sam's Boss: Sure.

Project Manager: As I understand it, what you want is a concise, accurate analysis in four days. Suppose Sam started with your task by creating a task outline that was detailed enough to let you know what the final analysis would look like and to guide the work of another analyst that Sam would handpick and would supervise. Once Sam got this analyst going, he'd split his time between working on my task and supervising the analyst working on yours. With a blueprint of what to do and Sam's regular supervision, your analysis would be completed and my project would get the attention it needs. Does that sound reasonable?

Sam's Boss: It sounds reasonable if Sam thinks it can be done successfully. So, Sam, what do you think?

Sam: Actually, I'd prefer doing it this way. The fun part is in the design of an analysis, not in the detail work that comes after.

Project Manager: It sounds as if we've got a solution. Wouldn't you agree?

Sam's Boss: Let's get after it!

In this smoother-than-life illustration, the influencer went through every step, from earning the right to closing. Your discussions may not be as hitch-free, but with a little planning and assertiveness, these steps can yield an improved outcome.

Step 4: Negotiate the Participant's Involvement

Occasionally, you'll hit a home run: The participant will return to the original plan and give you their full assistance. More often, a compromise like the one hammered out above is the wisest and easiest outcome to shoot for. Just remember, the key to negotiation is to look for a solution that satisfies your interests and the interests of the competing task. If you can enlist all the players in a creative discussion of interests, you'll have a good chance of finding that solution.

Step 5: Make People Happy

Always remember and never forget that whenever your attempts to influence a participant, a boss, a prime mover, or a stand-in have been completely or partially successful, you've been done a favor. Sure, you worked hard to build the original project plan and you put effort into getting the help that had already been promised to you. But if you want these people to support your projects in the future, make a point of thanking them in the present for their decision to reinstate your project's priority. And in addition, when the participant finishes their part of your project, go out of your way to thank them again. It's these small courtesies that make hard work easier and future tasks more likely to remain on schedule.

As difficult as it may be to produce the results of a project, they don't start producing value until they are received, understood, accepted, and used by the ultimate project customer. In the next chapter, we will learn how to make this all-important handoff.

Chapter 7

Presenting Project Results

*When communicating to a large or mass media audience,
I imagine I'm talking to a single person.*

—Red Barber, Sportscaster and Commentator

*If thou thinkest twice before thou speakest once, thou wilt
speak twice the better for it.*

—William Penn, founder of the colony of Pennsylvania

The good news was that after Jack finished his presentation to the end users, the inventory software upgrade project would be over. Of course, he'd learned a lot about planning and executing tasks, but not without much more work than he'd ever expected. Be that as it may, the upgrade software was all it needed to be, the end users were going to like it, and Jack could get on to other work.

The bad news was that to get to that "Promised Land," Jack would have to give a presentation to thirty or more people. Standing up in front of large groups while they all examined him was not Jack's idea of fun. In the past, Jack's stress level had gradually built up to a near panic attack by the day of the presentation. And the actual events, while never real meltdowns, had never yielded the audience appreciation Jack felt he deserved, considering the days of worry and work he had invested.

Nevertheless, a presentation was necessary, so Jack started writing his script and collecting transparencies. He wrote page after page, covering each detail of the software upgrade's features and functions. Transparencies were overflowing with supporting information that end users might need. As the presentation date inched closer, Jack began to realize that he would not have time to cover everything during the presentation, so he pulled together a handout packet to give people when they arrived. By presentation day, Jack had thirteen pages of script, forty-seven transparencies, and a churning hunk of burning funk at belly-button level.

The Strengths, Weaknesses, and Purpose of Presentations

Jack is about to experience another marginally successful presentation experience, marginal because he doesn't understand the purpose, the strengths, and the weaknesses of giving a presentation. For some strange reason, he thinks that his audience, in one sitting, can listen to, understand, integrate, and remember information that took him a week or more to compile. They can't. Their short-term memories aren't prepared to hold Jack's "core dump," and Jack's lecture approach to presenting doesn't give them any opportunity to process his information into their long-term memories. In addition to these organic limitations, they may not hear or understand parts of what he says because of naturally occurring periods of inattention that are almost entirely invisible to Jack.

Presentations are well suited for overviews, clarification, and motivation. In a well-designed presentation, audiences can see and understand the scope of a project or the resulting system or process so that, later, they will have a foundation from which they can study the details. Written reports or well-documented training sessions, but not conventional presentations, are a good way to convey moderate to large amounts of detail. With written reports, people can study large quantities of information when they have time. Training sessions with detailed support material provide the time needed for instructors and learners to discuss and practice information and skills.

Good presentations are the result of respecting the limitations of the medium, knowing what your audience needs and wants to hear, planning the presentation so that your message gets through, preparing supporting materials that amplify or clarify your message, and practicing enough so that you can present your material effectively while paying attention to your audience. During a presentation, unlike a lecture, two-way communication allows people the opportunity to ask clarifying questions. (If your idea of a presentation is a nonstop lecture, just send them your script to study.) Presentations can also be a very effective medium for encouraging people to adopt a process or system that they might otherwise resist.

Audience Analysis

Presenting to an unanalyzed audience is an act of faith that borders on foolishness (or masochism). Assuming that they are expecting what you've planned, that they are as interested as you are in the topic, that they have no objections or concerns (or that their concerns are the same ones you've identified), etc., etc., is foolish and disrespectful. You've asked that they invest their time in your presentation; if you don't go to the trouble to find out what they are likely to consider valuable, you're clearly communicating that you are willing to waste their time. You may not see it happening, but when the little voice inside any audience member's head starts saying "So what," their attention is probably going to turn to something else. If a chorus of "in the head" voices say "So what," their bodies might stay but their interest and involvement in what you're presenting will get right up and leave. Always remember and never forget that the audience came to have *their* wants and needs met—not yours! Unless you do a comprehensive audience analysis before you build your presentation, you invite disaster before you even begin (see Figure 7-1).

Who Is Your Real Audience?

Your real audience is made up of two groups: the people who must apply what they learn from your presentation to their work and/or the people who have a direct influence on your career. Your presentation goal must be to enable the first group to either use the outcome of your project when they leave or

Figure 7-1. Essentials of audience analysis.

1. Who are in the *real* audience?
2. What outcome does my audience expect?
3. What are my audience's experience and interest levels?
4. Does anyone in my audience have strong opinions about my topic (pro or con)?
5. How much time do I have?

study handouts without confusion or questions. If you succeed in this goal, the second group (career influencers) are going to be satisfied with your performance.

What Are They Expecting?

Before you prepare your presentation, call a few members of your real audience and ask, "What are you expecting to hear and learn from my presentation next Thursday?" If the answers of a small cross section of the audience are reasonable and uniform, you'll know where to begin your planning. But if your audience sampling reveals confusion or widely varying expectations, then you must (1) spend some time thinking about what you've heard, (2) write down an outcome agenda that you believe will provide the maximum benefit for the most people, and (3) massage it into a note/invitation telling audience members what to expect. The more uniform and accurate the audience's expectation is, the more they will be primed to listen and learn.

What Does the Audience Know and
How Interested Are They?

Dazed and confused audiences eventually nod off, so look out for these two common ways in which audience-insensitive presenters anesthetize their captives. In almost every case, you will know more about and be more interested in your presentation topic than anyone else in the room. Being comfortable with the presentation information can help you radiate confidence, but it can also cause you to ramble into Jargonland. To avoid talking over your audience's heads, gather advance information that will help you gauge their existing knowledge of and experience with your topic so that you can design your presentation with the appropriate amount of jargon and detail. The more diverse the group's background, the more careful you'll have to be to avoid confusing rookies who need the information.

Because you've been immersed in the topic for weeks or months, you may also be more interested in the topic than anyone else. Beforehand, ask questions of people who will give you a candid estimate of their interest level; then base the length of your presentation on how much the audience want and need to hear about your project's result. The more interested they are, the longer you can present. But if their interest level is low, consider giving a shorter presentation and putting more detail in handouts.

Are There Any Opinionated Audience Members?

While you're polling your audience for their average interest and knowledge levels, try to identify any potential bushwackers who might attend. Ask your prime mover if s/he knows about any politics that are impacting your project and ask some of your key end users for their read on how strong those ideas are and how resistant to change the people who hold them are. If your audience includes people who are opinionated, either pro or con, you're liable to get sometimes long-winded, problematic input.

A person with an ax to grind can turn your presentation into an argument. If one or more opinionated people are in your audience, execute a preemptive strike. Talk to them one-on-one before the presentation about their concerns. Since you'll spend the time anyway, it's better to argue out a point in private than to force your audience to watch you defend yourself and the results of your project during a presentation.

How Long Should You Speak?

Brevity is the soul of wit, and of presentations! With rare exceptions, audiences will applaud your decision to leave the kitchen sink at home. When you design your presentation, look at all the ground you could possibly cover and ruthlessly edit out aspects of your topic that are not absolutely necessary. Even if your prime mover tells you that you have all the time you need, plan to speak no longer than ninety minutes to two hours. There is a large neural pathway that runs from audience members' rear ends to their brains; at the ninety-minute to two-hour point, the rear end goes numb, followed closely by the seat of wisdom. Unless you're prepared to orchestrate a training experience with exercises, group work, and periodic breaks, accept the fact that when you run over two hours, you're pushing the tolerance limit of most audience members.

Designing Your Presentation

Some people, and perhaps even you, write their presentations down word for word. Not a good idea! Presenting is an oral event, not a written one. Spending precious preparation time slaving over a pencil or keyboard searching for just the right wording is useless unless you intend to read the presentation, which is never a good idea. When you present, you want to connect with an audience that is confident in your ability to provide them with value. You can't look your audience members in the eye and make that connection if you're reading at them or if you're tied to a set of detailed notes. Three things commonly happen when you read a presentation to an audience:

1. Members of the audience assume you don't know enough about your topic.
2. They become disconnected from you and the topic.
3. As their minds wander, they wonder why you didn't send them the notes rather than make them assemble in a room to listen to you read.

Defining Your Presentation Goal

When you analyzed your audience, you gathered information that will help you take the first step in developing your presentation: defining your presentation goal. Now it is time to crystalize that information into a very clear answer to the question, "What do I want my real audience [those people in attendance who must use the results of your project] to know, do, or believe when they leave my presentation?" Do you want them to know enough about your project result to go out and use it independently, or do you want them to believe that it is so valuable that they should study the user handout that you provide? Don't pull out a pencil and paper to create your goal; ponder the question as you drive to work, cook dinner, or mow your lawn. When you're finally clear about your goal, write the goal in the middle of a blank piece of paper so you can design the rest of the presentation around it.

Choosing the Key Presentation Elements

Your next step is to decide on essential elements: the facts, opinions, processes, actions, ideas, or benefits that the audience must hear, see, and understand in order to accomplish the presentation goal. For example, if your presentation goal is that the audience will believe that learning how to use a particular new software system is important to their productivity, essential elements may include testimonials from beta version users, encouragement from management, and projections of time savings. If your presentation goal is that the audience will know the sequence of input fields on each program screen when a new upgrade comes on-line, essential elements may include an illustration of the range of changes that will be involved, a demonstration of the new upgrade in action, and your answers to questions gathered beforehand from audience members.

Once you've thought through the essential elements that might be necessary to accomplish your goal, it's time to pull out the piece of paper with your goal in the middle. Draw a circle around your goal and surround it with notes indicating the essential elements (see Figure 7-2). Whenever possible, cluster related essential elements into quadrants around your goal.

Don't worry too much about evaluating the essential elements now; just capture them as if you were brainstorming. When you sense the inevitable "running out of gas" feeling coming on (you slow down, start repeating yourself, and/or dip into the obviously marginal), put your pencil down and make some decisions. As you look at the elements surrounding the goal, ask yourself, "If I could only present five of these, which ones would be absolutely essential to accomplishing my goal?" Circle the elements you selected, draw lines from each new essential element circle to the goal circle and erase all the unessential elements. You now have the basic outline for your presentation.

Figure 7-2. Essential elements for accomplishing the presentation goal.

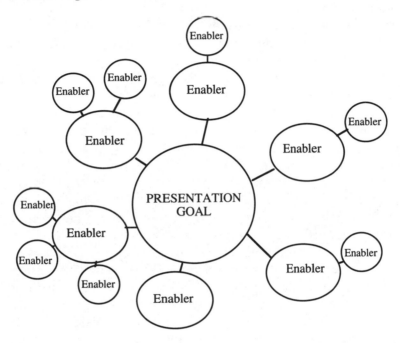

Creating the Outline in Two or More Sessions

You may want to create your presentation outline in more than one session. Brainstorm essential elements for twenty minutes, then put the paper away. Later on, pull the page out and consider combining elements, providing less experienced staff with more background, or offloading some information into a handout. Make the adjustments and put the page away again. If you approach the task of presentation design knowing you don't have to hammer it all out in one sitting, you'll start earlier, work smarter, and produce better results.

Choosing Your Words Carefully

With an overview of the presentation's goal and essential elements, but before you sequence the elements into a presentation, it's time to do some wordsmithing. The core of every essential element contains a key point that must be stated as clearly and understandably as possible. If your choice of words to communicate the key point of any essential element allows for more than one interpretation, your whole presentation goal is at risk. So carefully distill each key point into as few, very well chosen words as you can. For example, to drive home the fundamental belief of the essential element "The new version is easier to use than current version," your key point might be "The Phoenix credit form has fewer entry requirements and better instructions, making it significantly easier to use than the Delta credit form we are presently using." Because the words you use to express each key point are the most important in your presentation, you may want to take your list of key points to someone for review and feedback. If they have any questions about a key point (including "Hunh?"), rewrite until your points are crystal clear.

Now that you are entirely clear on your key points, you're ready to decide in what order you will present your essential elements. Although the way you sequence the content of your presentation will be, in large part, determined by the information you're presenting, you will also want to consider the workings of human memory. As a general rule, people remember what you say first and last better than what you say in the middle of a presentation. Therefore, begin with the essential element that your audience must remember. Thereafter, the only real requirement in sequencing is that there be a natural link from one essential element to another and that one topic expand into another in a way that the audience can understand and follow. Jumping around from topic to topic puts a great strain on any audience's willingness to listen and understand.

Essential Element Packets: Pathway to Clear Presentations

While each key point is central to its essential element, it can't stand on its own. Presentations are more than a series of key points. Each key point must be highlighted, supported, made relevant, and connected to what has been presented before. The seven components of an essential element packet are listed in Figure 7-3 and explained below.

Transition

There is always the risk that some of your audience members might get lost as you move from one essential element of your presentation to the next. If you've ever had the experience of thinking a presenter is talking about an earlier topic when all of a sudden you realize he's moved on without you, you understand just how possible this is, particularly if the topic is new or unfamiliar (or if you're working with three hours of sleep). A transition statement, such as "Moving on now to input screen layout," lets your audience follow your content more easily.

Attention Getter

In any audience, individual attention comes and goes. Caffeine kicks in and out, as do blood sugar, thoughts of home, worries about workload, etc. That's to be expected and accepted, with one exception. If you don't have the rapt attention of everyone in your audience immediately before you present each essential element's key point, you're likely to lose some people, putting your presentation goal at risk. Short, simple, and stimulating attention getters protect against that possibility.

Once you've transitioned, pause for an extra second, turn on a relevant visual, or say something like "If you remember one thing about our time together today, remember this. . . ."

Figure 7-3. Seven elements of an enabler packet.

1. Transition
2. Attention getter
3. Key points
4. Supporting evidence
5. Relevance statement
6. Summarizer
7. Key point sequel

The purpose of the attention getter is to rivet your audience onto your next words.

Key Points

State your key points clearly and simply. We've already covered key points; make 'em count!

Supporting Evidence

Supporting evidence is just that: facts, opinions, and data that make people believe, know, or be willing to act on the key point. If the key point is already well-known and well accepted, very little supporting evidence is required. On the other hand, if the key point is unfamiliar or resisted, considerable supporting evidence may be necessary. For example, if your key point tells the audience that a new safety requirement will actually be easier to comply with than the previous requirement, supporting evidence may take the form of graphs that contrast the time required by the old and new requirement, testimonial quotes from employees in other locations where the new requirement has been adopted, or a quick demonstration of the old and new requirement. Because presenters with a technical/quantitative background tend to overemphasize supporting evidence, sometimes at the expense of the key point itself, let's be clear on one thing: You need only enough supporting evidence to inform or convince your audience. Anything more and you run the risk of committing the ultimate sin, boring them.

Relevance Statement

"So what?" or "Why do I care about what you're talking about?" are the questions you ward off by including a relevance statement. If you aren't convinced that your entire audience understands why the key point is valuable to them, include a relevance statement such as, "So, as you can see, the new screen configuration will make it easier to avoid inputting mistakes and will save you considerable time because of the rework that can be avoided."

Summarizer

During the first few key points of your presentation, your audience will be able to remember what has gone before. But as you run longer and longer, your audience will retain more of the message if you make a practice of tying current points to past ones. Whether you do this orally ("The new screen configuration, in conjunction with the improved processing time, user-friendly interface, better memory utilization, and larger database capabilities begin to add up to an entirely upgraded package") or pictorially (using a transparency or flipchart), the assistance you provide for your audience's memory will enhance the impact of your presentation.

Key Point Sequel

The last element of the essential element packet is the key-point sequel ("So as you can see, the Phoenix credit form is significantly easier to use than the Delta credit form"). By restating the key point just before you end an essential element, you reinforce the basic message of the element and set up a natural jumping-off point for the transition to the next essential element packet.

Presentation Outline

Although your goal and essential element picture provided a helpful overview to select and sequence the building blocks of your presentation, this right brain approach to capturing information doesn't support the level of detail required by a fully developed presentation. As you build each essential element packet, you will be adding a great deal of information to your presentation in a carefully designed sequence. Capturing that information and sequence in an outline format as you build each packet will help you as you give your presentation.

With the exception of key points, your outline should be prepared as a set of cue words that remind you of the content you want to express. Select one or two important words that will remind you of the entire thought. Key points and key-point sequels should be written into your outline as you originally composed them in order to avoid the minor changes in wording that often happen when people work with cue words.

Develop your outline either on a word processor or on index cards so that you can easily edit and insert elements. You won't be building your presentation from start to finish, as you would present it, so you'll want enough flexibility in your outline medium to be able to insert the opening, comprehension check probes, and the closing after you've completed the essential element packets.

Opening and Closing a Presentation

With your presentation's content, length, and tone spelled out in some detail, you're ready to develop an appropriate opening and closing. Because your audience will form their opinion of you and what you have to say in the first couple of minutes of your presentation, it is important to delay designing your opening until you know enough about the presentation to design one that fits it well.

Your audience will accept you as you present yourself; if you're confident, clear, and compelling, they will quickly assume that what you have to say is important to them. But if you're nervous, unsure, and a little out of focus, your audience will be less receptive. Unfortunately, too many presenters underprepare their opening and, in some cases, try to figure one out while they're beginning the presentation. Given how much adrenaline is running through your veins when you begin a presentation, that approach is pretty risky. A much better tactic is to practice exactly what you're going to say until it's second nature. Program yourself so that you can say the words without really thinking. That way, after a ninety-second opening, your body chemistry will be getting back to normal and the audience will be impressed by your apparent calmness and organization.

Opening the Presentation

The best all-purpose opening for any presentation, the advance organizer, is composed of a few sentences that preview what you intend to present. Advance organizers presell the audience on the value of what they are about to experience and give them information that allows them to easily follow the presentation:

> *Project Manager:* During the next forty-five minutes, I am going to present the four key features of the upgraded inventory management system; input field improvements, processing changes, accessing changes, and newly available automatic reports. When we've finished, you will be able to use most of the functions of the new system independently and, with the help of a handout I'll provide, you'll be fully functional within a week.

Closing the Presentation

Does "Are there any questions?" sound familiar? Before we address productive ways to close a presentation, let's get clear on the profound downsides of this far too risky question. If you're tempted to declare open hunting season on yourself at the end of a presentation, you should be aware of the dangers you may encounter. First, most of your audience will be ready to leave as you wind down the presentation and will not welcome the opportunity to sit through your answers to someone who wasn't necessarily paying attention. Second, if a gadfly seizes "Are there any questions?" as an opportunity to argue points with you, the audience will leave your presentation remembering your off-the-cuff defense.

But third and most important, ending with "Are there any questions?" will deprive you of the opportunity to drive your presentation goal deep into their collective memories.

Because what they hear at the end of your presentation will be one of their best-remembered aspects of your presentation, ask them to go out and realize your goal:

> *Project Manager:* So, in conclusion, I'd like all of you to use the revised reporting system starting today. Thank you.

A carefully organized presentation that is seeded with carefully designed comprehension check probes (see below) won't require much Q&A.

If you're like most people who have become comfortable with "Are there any questions?" you're probably thinking that to end without fielding questions is a mistake; you'll send people off dissatisfied because they couldn't clear up some fuzziness about a key point. Admittedly, there are some occasions when ending with questions could be helpful to some audience members. But the downside of post-presentation Q&A is steep enough and consistent enough to persuade any presenter to resist the temptation. Instead, depend on your probes during a well-organized presentation to uncover confusion, and post your phone number for people to call you with their questions afterwards.

Probing Your Audience

Presentations, unlike speeches, involve give and take. Rather than proclaim what you want a monolithic audience to hear, a presenter tries to accomplish a know, do, and/or believe goal with a room full of individuals. That requires sending information to them as clearly and as compellingly as possible and receiving some indication that they understand and are willing to act. Sampling those two types of information from your audience requires asking probes at particular times throughout the presentation.

Look through your presentation outline for complex information, potentially contentious issues, new procedures, or vested interests. Wherever you find key points or supporting evidence that you think may elicit resistance or confuse people, develop an appropriately worded probe to find out if you've been clear and compelling. For example, after presenting the supporting evidence in a packet designed to convince a reluctant audience that a new system of work will save them time, you might ask, "John, would you agree that the new system represents an improvement in efficiency over the old one?" If John readily agrees and no one else takes the opportunity to express reservations, you can safely go on. But if John or any other audience member does have reservations, you can address and resolve them immediately rather than let him silently resist while you move on. Or perhaps you would probe an audience member after a demonstration with "Sally, have I been clear enough in my explanation of the input screens so that you feel you could navigate through one on your own?" If she replies positively, you can continue, but if she is still confused, you'll keep your audience with you by responding to their needs.

In addition to polling comprehension and agreement, you can also build probes into your presentation that will survey and stimulate an audience's willingness to act ("Saul, based on what I've presented so far, are you willing to change over to the new inventory process?" or "Frank, isn't this the biggest improvement in product tracking you've seen during your twelve years in accounting?").

Preparing and Presenting Visual Aids

The information that enters audience members' brains gets there through two senses, seeing and hearing. Studies of audience recall indicate that if you use only one of these senses, an audience will comprehend and recall less than if you use both seeing and

hearing. That means that for maximum impact, you must prepare and use visual aids.

Good visuals have impact: They promote retention, and
they support understandability. Among other things, that
means that copying pages from your handouts onto a clear
transparency probably won't cut it.

To create impact, do the following:

1. Edit key ideas down to phrases that get the point across.
2. Delete unnecessary words (complete sentences are not
   required).
3. Don't overload the visual with phrases (four to six are
   recommended).
4. Try to use a color(s) to make the visuals exciting and eye-
   pleasing.
5. Make sure there is a sharp contrast between the words
   and the background.
6. Start each word on the visual with a capital and use low-
   ercase letters for the rest of the word. The capital letter
   will cue the reader to each new word, which makes rapid
   reading much easier.

Retention is influenced by the amount of information on a
visual and by its colors, shapes, borders, and fonts. If your visuals all share the same format, your audience will have a hard
time distinguishing one from the other. Unfortunately, many
corporations and individuals generate visuals that look exactly
alike except for the words on them. They may look "better,"
but they are much less effective in gluing your points to your
audience's memory.

To support understandability, choose your words carefully;
they should be as basic as possible without making it seem that
you're talking down to your audience. Do not use jargon. It is
not only confusing in its own right; it might quickly turn off
your audience. If you find that a particular point requires lots of
explaining to be understood, break the point down into a few
visuals rather than try to get everything onto one.

Whenever possible, prepare all your visuals beforehand.
The time you spend writing a visual for your audience on a

flipchart is time spent with your back to them. In a similar vein, don't read your visual to the audience. You don't want to give the audience the impression that you think they can't read.

The purpose of a visual is to aid the presenter, not the other way around. The visual should complement what you're saying, not duplicate it. Know your visuals well enough so you can make the same point with different words. That way, your audience can duplex the information, taking it in visually and auditorily at the same time.

Preparing Yourself

The difference between an adequate presentation and a really good one is usually determined by whether the presenter takes the time to prepare him- or herself so s/he can deliver the presentation with all the focus, clarity, and ease s/he's capable of. Just as a great musical composition can be butchered by a musician who hasn't practiced adequately, a well-designed presentation can be diminished by a presenter who tries to deliver it cold.

Recruit people for a tryout audience who are as unfamiliar with the content of your presentation as the least experienced person you expect in your real audience. Avoid choosing co-workers for your presentation tryout because they are likely to unconsciously fill in gaps in your content. A naïve tryout audience is much more helpful because they will become confused when you aren't clear and will tell you.

Deliver your complete presentation just as you would give it to you final audience and then ask for specific feedback. Ask questions like:

"What confused you?"

"Where did I fail to convince you?"

"Did I lose you at any point?"

"Were there areas where you definitely disagreed with me?"

"Did you walk away from the presentation knowing something new, believing something different, or willing to take action?"

Take careful notes, upgrade your presentation, and practice. With this much focused work under your belt, you'll know your presentation well enough to pay lots of attention to individual audience reactions, make extemporaneous adjustments based on probe answers, and finish on time.

Avoiding Nervousness

If giving a presentation makes you nervous, relax; you're in good company. *The Book of Lists* regularly includes an accounting of what people fear, and, while fear of death typically hovers around the number three rank, giving presentations usually appears as number one.

To reduce their nervousness about an upcoming presentation, many people try shutting it out of their minds; they neither think about it nor prepare for it. But as the presentation date gets closer and closer, the defenses of procrastination eventually break down and the terrifying prospect of getting in front of a group looms. For many panicky presenters, that means pulling the presentation together the day before and hoping for the best. But how can you be at your best when you have to deliver a hastily prepared presentation? You can't. So you wrestle your way through the experience, adding one more reason to become nervous the next time you must give a presentation.

What we have here is a nervousness trap. Apprehension fuels procrastination. Procrastination minimizes preparation. Minimal preparation leads to marginal audience acceptance and reactions. And lackluster audience responses fuel apprehension about presentations. To become a better presenter, you must break this chain somewhere, and where better than at the beginning, with nervousness?

What to Do

When you are told or realize that you must give a presentation, whip out this book and your scheduler. Set milestones for each phase of presentation development and give the milestones teeth by meeting with your boss to show her your schedule and development plan. Block out specific parcels of time to work on meeting your milestones. Persuade your boss to pencil in time to attend and critique your run-through.

Videotape your run-throughs. Then look at and listen to yourself. You will not only see places where the presentation isn't working; with repeated viewings you will also become less self-conscious (not to mention finding the motivation to finally go on that diet you've been putting off).

If you are really nervous, even after all your preparation, sit yourself down and have the following chat with yourself:

> "I am not and am not expected to be perfect. My success and the success of my presentation does not rely on every person in the room liking me or what I'm saying. Because I'm well prepared, the best way to do well in this presentation is to enjoy talking to these people and providing them with something valuable. So that's what I'm going to do."

Before and during the presentation, make a conscious effort to breathe slowly and deeply. Most nervous people breathe rapidly and shallowly, which makes presentations they give sound breathy and makes it hard for their audience to listen. If you consciously breathe more deeply, you'll speak more clearly and you'll feel calmer. Avoid hand-wringing, shoulder hunching, and any other nervous physical behavior. Instead, focus on relaxing. Lowering your shoulders and loosening your hands will allow your body to send your brain an "I'm relaxed" message. And, in the same vein, smile from the inside out at people. It'll cause them to smile at you, which, because of the lifetime of experience you've had with happiness and smiling, will convince you that you're having fun.

Handouts

As a general rule, giving people handouts of your presentation before you present it only encourages them to read instead of listen. The only exception to this rule is a very sparse outline. With some advance information about the topics you're going to hit and a lot of white space to take notes, you can help people pay attention and you can short-circuit questions that will be answered later in your talk.

Dedicated, hardworking project managers frequently fall into the trap of thinking that the goal of their project is to produce the result they targeted in the project plan. That's not true. The goal of a project is to realize the value of that result. That means you must take the final step: putting the result into the hands of an accepting, enthusiastic, knowledgeable group of end users. And the only way you can do that with confidence is by personally presenting the result to them in a highly effective presentation. Don't drop the ball when you're five yards from the goal line.

Chapter 8

Managing People and Projects: The Psychology of Project Shelving

Big projects give people something to identify with and work toward.

—Frank Carlucci, U.S. National Security Adviser

The world breaks everyone and afterwards many are strong at the broken places.

—Ernest Hemingway, American novelist

Jack looked through the metal grate on his window to the neatly manicured lawn that greeted newcomers to the Institute. He liked having a view. For the first couple of weeks, he had been confined to a special room so he couldn't hurt himself. Back then, in the "bad time," Jack saw only his wife and an occasional medication nurse. Now, he was allowed to get up and move around. Twice a day, he could go out to the day-room and play cards with the other patients. Things were better, and like the blossoming flowers outside his window, Jack was beginning to unfold again.

Jack's unfortunate "snap" happened just a week before he was supposed to present the inventory software upgrade. Long hours and mounting anxiety about his presentation were beginning to take their toll; after five smoke-free years, Jack embraced Joe Camel and washed the smoke down with massive quantities of coffee.

On a particularly tense morning, Fran arrived unannounced to tell Jack that the software upgrade had to be shelved so he could begin on a new database formatting project immediately. For a second, Jack just looked at Fran with the blank expression of uncomprehending disbelief. "No, you're kidding, right? Tell me you're kidding!" Jack pleaded.

Somewhat surprised by the intensity of Jack's denial, Fran just looked back at him for a second. She finally replied in a matter-of-fact tone, "No, Jack. I'm really not kidding. We'll get around to the inventory upgrade launch eventually, but right now, priorities have changed and we need you on this database immediately."

During the silence that followed, Fran could have sworn she heard the sound of bacon frying on a hot skillet. *Fsssst. Pop.* Then the sound of a terminal crashing against the wall behind her mobilized Fran as she ran for cover. In seconds, Jack transformed his neatly organized office into a junkyard of broken equipment. Screaming "I'm not going to take this anymore!" Jack had found, in one defining moment, that point beyond which his strength could not take him.

Jack cracked for many reasons that we will not know and for some reasons that you probably share with him. Some of the same factors that make a person good at project leadership (achievement orientation, organization, attention to details, identification with one's job, etc.) can make him or her vulnerable to the personal pain of project shelving. This final chapter cannot change the pressures you will face during projects you lead or projects that you must abort before they can go full-term. But perhaps, it can help you better understand yourself and your feelings and can arm you with tactics that can keep your project alive.

Why Does Project Shelving Feel So Bad?

We're all adults. We all know that priorities change and that the ability to seize opportunities makes organizations profitable and stable. So why all this hubbub about shelving one project in favor of another? It's not as if our inability to finish a particular project were going to result in a smaller paycheck. As a well-adjusted, mature team player, you just shift gears, zooming into a new direction as smoothly as a race car driver negotiates a hairpin turn. Right? Wrong! As much as superficial logic would suggest that dropping one project for another should be easy, it isn't—and for some very good reasons. To understand why project shelving isn't easy, we first have to consider some of the basic tenets of human nature that drive the behavior and reactions of every hardworking contributor.

According to the fundamental principles of behavioral psychology, people behave in the ways they do because their particular behaviors, reactions, and abilities have been reinforced in the past, making them more likely to occur in the present and future. As the strength of a behavior increases, the chances of its being reinforced again increase; when you have more of a particular behavior, you have more opportunity to reinforce it. So, if working hard at school is reinforced with praise and A's, working hard becomes more and more likely to happen. And, as it becomes more likely, the chances of its being rewarded increase. Over time, what happens to kids who are consistently reinforced for hard work is that they become persistent, hard-working students who can succeed at tasks of ever-increasing complexity.

Sounds great, doesn't it? A dozen or more years of adequate instruction, regular feedback, and consistent praise and you can grow yourself an achievement-oriented adult. And that's just what happens. Every year, high schools and colleges graduate a crop of achievement-oriented people who are eager to move out of the developmental hothouse into the "real world." Little do they know!

Schools view their mission as one of developing capable, hardworking people who can contribute to society and enjoy a self-sufficient, productive life. To do that, we have created an artificial environment called "school" in which tasks are clearly defined, feedback is systematic, and praise for success is the norm. No wonder we call it an ivory tower.

Programmed with a history of recognition for achievement, waves of capable people enter a workforce that is all too real. Now, instead of getting an A for a job well done, employees get a paycheck for putting in two weeks of work. The semester never ends, grades are not posted, and praise is much less common. This can be a big shock to the motivation system.

Which brings us to "extinction," a technical term in behavioral psychology that describes the process of weakening behavior by withholding reinforcers that had, in the past, been provided. If the previously reinforced behavior is strong, it will persist for quite a while without any reinforcers. But as a new history of nonreinforcement is written, the behavior will gradually diminish either to zero or to a very low level. And while his or her behavior is weakening, the person who is experiencing extinction will also engage in emotional behaviors that are typical of "burnout" or "stress-out." Because most achievement-oriented people in work settings don't experience complete extinction (some peer or boss recognition occurs), the extinction-caused reduction in enthusiasm and focus can go on for years, with manageable feelings of fatigue and "what's the use" instead of full-blown emotional outbursts. But without praise or recognition for work on tasks or projects, what was once an exciting challenge becomes another boring or demanding or stressful or meaningless or dreadful—pick one—day of work drudgery or misery or mind-numbing frustration or abuse—pick another one.

Enter the achievement-oriented project leader, working away at the project she has gradually come to identify with; this isn't just a project; it's her project. She has invested energy, experience, and focus in the project and fully expects to complete it. Until her boss tells her that due to priority changes, she will have to shelve that project so she can work on a new one. Not only is she busy coping with the ongoing effects of a seriously reduced schedule of reinforcement for hard work, but now the time and effort already invested in the present project is abruptly zeroed out. No recognition during the project, and now no recognition when it's over. It's tough to be on a diet, but it gets even tougher when you're forced to skip your can of SlimFast™, too.

If extinction is equivalent to going on a motivation diet, frustration is when someone swipes a regularly scheduled meal. Somewhere along the way to getting something you want (recognition for finishing a project, getting a promotion for diligent work, or a trophy for coming in first in a race), something happens to keep you from getting it (your boss shelves the project, someone from outside is given the job, or you twist your ankle). Where the feeling of extinction is generally one of burnout, fatigue, depression or "the blues," frustration triggers internal or external anger. We've all seen the external anger of tantrums, abuse, and highway honking, but the internal anger is more subtle. Withdrawal is a common response to a frustrating situation. You stew in your own juices as you move from one project to the next, which you must assume may not have any more chance of making it to completion than the one you just shelved.

Task shelving feels so bad because, in the midst of a "recognition diet," your personal identification with accomplishments that define much of your worth are discounted by someone else's new priority. Intense, goal-directed efforts are being stopped dead in their tracks because someone somewhere else in the company changed priorities without even discussing them with you. And there is little else you can do but comply.

What Can You Do to Reduce Bad Project-Shelving Feelings?

Because the nature of and rules for work have changed so much (and will continue to change), people who work must make some adjustments. Because the only person you can reliably influence is yourself, there is only one person who can and must make those adjustments—you. So pick up the new weapons that will help you protect your project from abrupt shelving and/or strap on the psychological armor that will protect you from lethal project-related frustration.

How to Reduce the Likelihood of Shelving

1. *Regularly resell your prime mover.* You can't assume that your project priority will remain high indefinitely. Competing needs and new opportunities can spawn new projects that will vie for the resources your project is presently enjoying. This being true, keeping your project's priority high requires some "managing up": making sure that your prime mover is well informed about the benefits s/he can expect from your project.

If you proactively find new ways to keep your prime mover regularly convinced that your project will yield many and/or big benefits, s/he is much less likely to become attracted to another, newer project. Both in person and via memo, make a point of keeping your prime mover up to speed and excited.

2. *Keep your projects as short as possible.* As a general rule, the longer your project, the more likely it is to be shelved in favor of one that is more pressing. So, whenever possible, try to keep your project time requirements to a minimum; that way, there is a smaller window of interruption and a greater willingness to wait the short period until you become available.

3. *Front-load the resources needed for your project.* The more resources people have invested in a project, the less likely they are to bail out without any return on their investment. So, whenever possible, try to buy needed equipment or involve "valuable" others as early as you can.

4. *Regularly probe your prime mover for competing projects.* Being blindsided is one of the most frustrating aspects of most project shelvings. If you have advance information that points toward a possible shelving, you can try to resell your project and you can prepare for the possibility of an interruption. Probe the prime mover regularly with questions like, "Are there any new projects on the horizon that people are pushing to start?" or "Do you see any problems with launching this project product next month as planned?"

How to Adjust Your Sensitivity to Frustration

1. *Work on more than one project at a time.* The more you have invested in any single project and the more you see your leadership role in a single project as important to your prestige, the more frustrating it is when the project is shelved. So try to keep a couple of projects active simultaneously. You will not only be protected against the feelings of loss that accompany project shelving, you'll also be able to maintain interest in multiple projects more easily.

2. *Work on enriching other aspects of your life.* People who experience the most intense response to project-shelving frustration tend to depend on work as the primary and sometimes sole source of input and validation. On the other hand, people with a well-developed family life, hobbies, and a network of friends can often withstand the frustrations of shelving more easily. Take stock of where, how, and with whom you spend your life and, if your analysis suggests that you're too narrowly focused on work, set some life-expansion goals, prioritize them, and get after them!

3. *Adjust your expectations.* Part of frustration is being blocked from getting what you firmly expect you can and should get. The stronger the expectation, the more intense the emotional response will be if your expectations are not realized. When you start a new project, you probably have the unstated expectation that you'll be able to complete it without interruption. Since experience tells us that an out-of-the-blue interrup-

tion is quite possible, try beginning each new project with the statement, "I expect to be able to work on this project either until I'm done or until something more important requires my valuable attention." If you can get that more realistic expectation firmly planted, shelving will be easier to take, should it happen.

4. *Adjust your beliefs.* Albert Ellis, a well-known American psychologist, proposed that a great deal of stress comes from the conflict between some of our basically unrealistic beliefs and what really happens. For example, if you believe that you must be perfect and unfailingly competent in all that you undertake (one of the top ten unrealistic beliefs Ellis's research uncovered among Americans), any sign of failure is going to trigger a stress response. Or if you believe that you must have approval and acceptance from every adult (another top ten belief), signs of rejection or even apathy will trigger a stress response. As it turns out, plenty of achievement-oriented project leaders carry both of these irrational (as in "not reasonable") beliefs around. And if one of those beliefs is double-crossed with the directive to shelve one project in order to work on another, they are very likely to react to that as an indication of disrespect and/or as a vote of no-confidence for their competency.

Most people don't spend much time thinking about what they really believe and consequently don't put much effort into adjusting nice-sounding but unworkable beliefs. If you are a hardworking, achievement-oriented project manager, chances are that you've got some potentially stress-inducing beliefs you should consider changing. If you are one of those people who do take project shelving as a personal rebuke, consider adopting more realistic beliefs, like "I'm most valuable when my skills are being applied to the most pressing projects. I depend on my boss and others who have the big picture to help deploy my abilities for maximum impact."

5. *Carefully document your project on a daily basis.* Part of the frustration of project shelving comes from the reality that once shelved, a project can take a lot of time and effort to restart. Much of the restart effort involves re-creating the conditions that existed without benefit of accurate and complete documentation. By building documentation activities into your normal

project management work, you are always ready for an orderly shelving and for an efficient restart.

As the pace of business competition continues to pick up throughout the rest of this decade, the need to balance focus and flexibility will continue to increase. Difficult challenges requiring the planning, focus, coordination, efficiency, and forethoughtfulness that are at the heart of project work are presenting themselves more quickly than ever before. To succeed rather than be overwhelmed, we must continuously improve our ability to choose the right challenges, respond to them efficiently, and make adjustments as circumstances require. Your enthusiasm and understanding will have much to do with the success you enjoy as you meet the future.

Index

meetings
  for consensus building, 46–47
  for delegating project mile-
    stone, 25
  for project plan review, 69–72
memory, and presentation order,
    140
mentors, input to planning, 43–44
milestones
  in daily planner, 101
  deadlines for, 26
  of delegated projects, 24
  dependencies on, 55
  developing trail of, 47–50
  explaining in initial project re-
    view, 80–81
  in flowcharts, 61
  and problem solving, 68
  and schedule maintenance, 50
  scheduling time to review, 103
  specifications for, 25
  in time management, 95–98
mind, 31
mistakes, in coaching, 39–40
monitoring, 26–27
motivation for project, 5–6

neatness in flowchart creation, 65
negotiating, participant involve-
    ment, 128
nervousness, avoiding in presen-
    tations, 150–151

objections in persuasion, 117–119
opening of presentations, 144–145
open office architecture, 106
open probes, 13
  rehearsing, 16
opinionated members of audi-
    ence, 136
opinions, from probes, 13

outline, for presentation, 139,
    143–144
overview of information, 13

participants, *see* influencing parti-
    cipants; project participants
peers, 115
perfection, 94
perfectionists, 68
performance, ability of helpers, 23
periodic project reviews, 78,
    85–86
  schedule creation, 82
  scheduling planning, 103
personal work preferences, and
    scheduling, 103
persuasion
  psychology of, 30–36
  tactics of, 117–119
  of willing but unable, 28–36
phone calls, timing for, 101
physical skills, coaching, 38
planned questions, 13
planning, 27, 41–72
  brainstorming in, 51–53
  for coaching, 37
  commitments from participants
    in, 50–51
  for delegated projects, 25
  goals in, 44–47
  inventory of necessary re-
    sources and approvals in,
    53–54
  milestone trail development,
    47–50
  need for, 43–44
  see also charting
politics, 9, 136
power, 115
practice
  of mistakes, 39
  for presentation, 144, 149–150